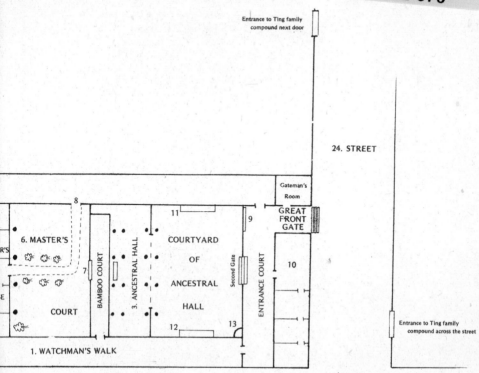

Entrance to Ting family
compound next door

24. STREET

Gateman's
Room

GREAT
FRONT
GATE

8

6. MASTER'S

R'S

11

9

COURTYARD

OF

ANCESTRAL

HALL

Second Gate

7

BAMBOO COURT

3. ANCESTRAL HALL

ENTRANCE COURT

10

E

COURT

12

13

1. WATCHMAN'S WALK

Entrance to Ting family
compound across the street

To Ting Family Cemetery

8. Little Convenient Gate—for the Master's use from the Master's Court to the Eastern Watchman's
       Walk.
9. Spirit Screen.   Not a separate wall but built into the wall facing the Great Front Gate.
0. Carpenter's shop.   Was reception room when used by the Ting family.
1. Boxwood Terrace and 12. Juniper Terrace.
                 These were on either side of the Courtyard of the Ancestral Hall which was
                 paved with bricks laid in "everlasting" pattern, with wh   pebbles in the spaces.
3. Baptistry.
4. Kitchen, two bays, with pantry the third bay.
5. House used as laundry and also sleeping quarters for the washman-table boy.
6. House of Those Who Must Also be Cared For. Still left in the original five bays. Used as dor-
                 mitory when Mother ran a boy's boarding school.
7. Kangs, the original brick beds in the rooms.
8. House of Mr. Tsang, the headmaster. Also three bays.
9. Three bays where Dada and her husband, the cook, lived until the boarding school was started and
                 they moved to the village.
0. Room with mill in it, the mill stone turned by a donkey.
1. Ramp up from the highway, paved with field stone.
2. Entrance to dye shop, to whom the Ting family next door had rented their farm yard. Their
                 compound was identical to ours.
3. Gate into the courtyard where Mr. Chu, Father's teacher, and family lived.
4. Street, paved down the middle with worn millstones and on the sides with fieldstone.

A CHINA CHILDHOOD

Chinese Materials Center, Inc.

Asian Library Series No. 10

A CHINA CHILDHOOD

by
Ida Pruitt

with a foreword by
John K. Fairbank

CHINESE MATERIALS CENTER, INC.

SAN FRANCISCO

1978

© Copyright 1978 by Chinese Materials Center, Inc.

ISBN 0-89644-523-2

PRINTED IN THE REPUBLIC OF CHINA

CONTENTS

ILLUSTRATIONS

(facing p. 86)

The Pruitt Family Compound (*front endpaper*)

1. Author's father, C.W. Pruitt, in his twenties (sometime in the 1880's)

2. Father's teacher

3. Father's teacher's wife, who bore fifteen children and raised five

4. Chao Teh-shan, the herd boy who became an official

5. Author and brother riding in baskets on a donkey

6. Mule-litter—usual mode of travel for any distance

7. The family starting to P'eng-lai

Rough Sketch of Sung-chia-tan Village (*rear endpaper*)

FOREWORD

THIS ENTRANCING STORY IS deceptively simple. A little American girl, daughter of missionaries, grows up in a Chinese village in Shantung province not far from the Yellow Sea. The time is late in the nineteenth century. The narrator shows you every detail of the household and its people—the orderly architectural layout of the compound and its several courtyards, the adjustments made by the foreign family living conscientiously in Chinese style, the way they and their servants perform their various roles. With her Chinese nurse, a peasant woman, the little girl explores the carefully structured life around her in the compound. Growing older, she ventures out into the village and eventually into the countryside.

Suddenly one realizes that this concrete, bit-by-bit narrative has taken one across a cultural gap into another way of life that is now gone, that of old China. Up to the age of twelve when her story stops, the little girl has grown up more Chinese than American. She has learned to see the world through the eyes of the nurse and of the Chinese community around her.

Very early, for example, she becomes aware of her parents' intrusive foreignness as they try to Christianize their Chinese neighbors. Moving into this ancient Chinese house, they take out the latticework and substitute "aggressive vertical windows of the West. . . . The paper that had covered the lattice, that had let in the soft light and kept out the heat and the cold and people's vision, was replaced with glass, hard and cold, that had to be defended with curtains." Her American parents also rearranged the furniture but, says the little girl, "I never felt comfortable with the arrangement of the room. . . . The Chinese way would have been much more formal." Within the high compound walls, her mother felt "caged, confined," but for the daughter they provided "dignity, formality, and privacy." Later she found that "the roofs in America had no dignity and often the rooms were not of harmonious dimensions."

The Hall of the Ancestors in this ancient house was naturally converted by the missionaries into their church. The little girl saw it as a mutilation. In one corner of the courtyard they had dug a hole to make a baptistry which could be filled with water. "When dry the hole was ugly and gaping. . . . I did not like to look at that hole. Even the thought of it hurt me. . . . Father's face would be beautiful as he raised a new member, symbolically, from death to life. To me, however, it was a grotesque and somewhat indecent ceremony, performed in a pit that had broken the harmony of the court."

Baptism in her eyes was merely initiation into the club, for the little girl soon realized that the Chinese communicants "thought of the church as a club. The Chinese word chosen by the early missionaries was *hui*, club, organization, assembly. The Baptists were the *Chin Hsin Hui*, the Club of the Immersed Believers. . . . The nearest analogy to church membership was the trade guild and the secret society."

The narrator is Ida Pruitt, who grew up in a village near the town of P'eng-lai in Shantung. Later she went to a girls' school in Georgia and to Teachers College at Columbia and eventually into social work in Philadelphia and later at the Massachusetts General Hospital in Boston. There she worked with a pioneer of hospital social service, Ida M. Cannon. Returning to her native China, Miss Pruitt became head of the Hospital Social Service Department in the Peking Union Medical College. For twenty years, until the Japanese invasion of 1937-38, she put her training in this new field to use in dealing with the manifold social problems of the patients at this great Rockefeller-supported hospital.

Speaking Chinese with her native Shantung accent, instinctively aware of the nuances of Chinese behavior, Miss Pruitt became a unique interpreter of Chinese life, sought after by sinologists and social investigators. The book by Olga Lang, *Chinese Family and Society* (New Haven: Yale University Press, 1946), owed much to her detailed case files. Confronting people's day-to-day problems, she developed an interest in the written record of everyday life in China. In 1936 she published a translation of a vivid story, *The Flight of an Empress, told by Wu Yung, whose other name is Yü-ch'uan, transcribed by Liu K'un* (Yale University Press, 1936), a valuable first-person account of how a local magistrate met the Boxer year and its aftermath. During two years in Peking she also had long conversations three times a week with an old lady from her native P'eng-lai, a peasant grandmother who had seen the gamut of hardship in her time. The resulting volume was *A Daughter of Han: The Autobiography of a Chinese Working Woman, from the story told her by Ning Lao T'ai-t'ai* (Yale University Press, 1945), a unique contribution to our understanding of the personal vicissitudes of Chinese life in the late nineteenth century.

More than most Westerners who have lived there, Ida Pruitt left her heart in Peking. Her attachment to China is deeply inbred. It relates to the whole balance of life, the values, satisfactions, and restraints of the ordered Confucian society. This is why her story of the colors and textures, the discoveries and attachments of childhood, give us such insight into a culture now hidden by time and distance.

John K. Fairbank

PREFACE

"OF THE MAKING OF many books there is no end" was said ages ago by a man long considered wise. That I should add to the spate daily coming off our presses seemed to me an unnecessary occupation. Two considerations changed my mind. Now that so many people are called upon to live in two or even more ways of life at the same time, it seemed to me that perhaps my childhood, lived in two very distinct patterns, would be of interest. And second, the old China in which I spent my childhood is no more. That its old ways may be of interest to students and even others I felt possible. Although the old ways have passed into history, the basic character of the people is still there: their independence (some call it the stubbornness of the peasant), their sense of fair play, their never-ending diligence, their sense of rhythm and harmony, and their dignity.

IDA PRUITT

xiii

IN THE BEGINNING

THE LITTLE GIRL LEANED against the pole of the mule litter at rest in a Chinese courtyard. When the litter was slung on the backs of the mules the poles rode chest high to a man but were not more than a foot and a half above the ground when the frames that went over the wooden saddles straddled on the ground. The little girl leaning against the pole could not have been more than a year and some months old, a year and a half.

She pulled her hand along the pole. A roughness in the surface pricked her finger and hurt her. She looked at the pole and felt again its hardness and roughness. She looked at the finger and at the scratch and looked again at the pole which had hurt her. It was hard and alien. "This is not me," she thought with surprise.

She lifted her head and looked out into the courtyard. Huge blue figures loomed and moved and were unfocused shapes in the distance that meant nothing. More

1

"not me." How much "not me" there was.

The rest of her life was to be spent in learning about "me" and "not me," in trying to understand them both in ever widening circles—of experience, of thought, and of understanding, widening ever outward like the circles curving away from a stone dropped into a pond.

Not only, however, was the "me" and the "not me" to be sorted out. There were also for the little girl the patterns of two very dissimilar ways of life from which to choose her habits and her thoughts. Perhaps it was not to choose between them, but to take something from each.

Why was this child with brown hair, green eyes, and a fair complexion, obviously of Western European ancestry, dressed as a Chinese, her hair combed into two straight braids that stood out from either side of her head? Why was she pricking herself into consciousness of life outside herself, the knowledge that she was not the universe or even the center of it, as she leaned against the pole of a mule litter in a Chinese courtyard?

The answer lay with her parents who had followed the urge that had been with the people of Western Europe ever since the dawn of history, the urge to go West and ever further West.

A farm boy in North Georgia heard a returned missionary tell about the "heathen Chinese" and hellfire. Dimly, through the exhortations of the missionary, the tales of poverty, disease, and corruption, he had glimpsed the beauty of the Chinese people and their culture, which he was to see, understand, and to love, and he knew that these people must not be left to hellfire. Hellfire was very real in North Georgia in those days. The boy had his call to the ministry and went to China in 1882 (one of the first to cross the country by rail and sail from San Francisco instead of going around the Horn), a missionary of the Southern Baptist Convention.

A young woman in Ohio, teaching school in California in 1887, read the letters from a cousin preaching the Gospel in a Presbyterian Mission in Peng-lai, Shantung Province, in North China, and thought that was the place to take her restless soul. One morning, in P'eng-lai, as she was studying the Chinese language, as all new missionaries must, she answered the doorbell. There stood a blue-eyed Chinese. The clothes, the long blue gown, and the short sleeveless black jacket were Chinese, even the shaven head which meant he had a queue, the round melon-section skull cap, and the black cloth shoes; but the eyes were blue, more blue than any eyes she had ever seen, and the mustache had a hint of bronze in it. Then she knew. He was the widower from the Baptist Mission who had been "out in the field" when she had arrived.

In three months they were married. They moved from P'eng-lai, in the prefecture of Tengchow, where there were several families of missionaries, to the village of Sung-chia-tan in the Huang-hsien district, where for most of these years they were the only Westerners. The little girl was born, however, in P'eng-lai, within the walled city, in the house where her father had lived his first six years in China. There was no Western trained physician in Huang District and it did not seem sensible for the one busy doctor in P'eng-lai to leave his patients for a woman to begin labor.

So it was that the little girl was born in a Chinese house, in a Chinese compound, in a Chinese city, the walls of which had first been laid down in the time of the

first emperor of the Ch'in Dynasty, two hundred years
before Christ, and which had been an imperial city (as the
triple-roofed gate towers testified) in the time of Yang Ti
of the Sui Dynasty, in the seventh century A.D. When she
was a month old, they took her back to Huang District
and when she was a hundred days old they gave her the
"Hundred-Year-Old" birthday party usually given only to
boys. Her parents wanted to show that in Christian countries girls were as precious as boys. They knew that in
this old civilization of farmers and artisans the son was
the only hope for support in sickness and old age and in
the life to come, and that daughters, married off to other
families, took with them all that had been invested in
them. But ancestor worship was wrong, the parents believed, and women should learn skills and be able to work
as well as men. The parents belonged to the world of
the industrial revolution. Furthermore, they did not
admit to themselves that in their own country also a man
child was more desired, usually, than a girl. All the church
members came to the party and put around the little girl's
neck a silver chain with a heavy silver lock such as was
given boys to lock them to this world. But the little girl
never remembers seeing it. It probably found its way to
some missionary society in an American church.

2

A HOUSE IS AN OUTER SELF

AFTER THAT EARLIEST MEMORY, as I stood beside the mule litter in the farm courtyard, there is no single memory in my mind until my sixth year. Throughout those first years, however, there was etched on my mind, line upon line, laid in my heart, layer upon layer, painted in my heart and in my mind, brush stroke after brush stroke, that compound where we lived and the people in it and the people who came to it. This was my world.

A house is an outermost covering, more permanent than the clothes we wear and more permanent to the Chinese families of that time, who lived for generations in one house, than the flesh and bones of their bodies. One would be naked without a house. Chinese stories of life in the past centuries often start with the story of the house in which the people lived, and the relationship of the people to that house. Therefore, as I was born in the last century and lived in a Chinese house, that house

5

and my relationship to it and to the people in it and those who came to it must first be described.

We lived in a compound made up of seven courtyards and the eleven one-story houses of those courtyards. The main house of a courtyard was always on the north side and faced south to get the life-giving sunshine. The smaller houses were sometimes against the east wall and sometimes against the west wall. This left the courtyard space as solid a whole as possible. A high wall surrounded the whole compound, broken on the south by the Great Front Gate and on the north by the Great Back Gate. The compound was as long as a small city block and almost half as wide.

A compound was laid out to serve all the needs of a Chinese family of that time. It was a place for the family to sleep, eat, talk, enjoy the flowers and the sunshine; for the ancestors to return to at stated intervals; where with due regard to hierarchy and as much as the income of the family allowed, provision was made for all sides of living. A family tried to do as much of its work as possible within its own gates.

On entering the Great Front Gate, with the gate-keeper's room on the right, one came to the Entrance Court with reception rooms and offices. Then came the Courtyard and Hall of the Ancestors. After that were the three courtyards and their houses where the family lived. Then the Farm Courtyard and the Great Back Gate, with the Threshing Floor beyond. Each courtyard was separated from all other parts of the compound by walls.

The pattern for the layout of the compound was developed over the centuries, over the millennia. The foundations of a capital city of the Shang Dynasty (fifteenth to eleventh centuries B.C.) dug up by archeologists of the 1930s, showed a strong likeness to the ground plan of our houses. Architects and the Masters of Wind and Water, the geomancers, the wise who studied the old books, knew how houses should be built. They had developed the plan that suited the needs of the people of China through the great era of the farming and handicraft way of life. I lived in such a compound at the end of that long era in China.

Compounds were of many sizes. The house of a peasant or city laborer was a single courtyard with a three-*chien* house across the width of the courtyard and against the north wall. A *chien* is the space between the pillars holding up the roof and is constant in the relationships of height, width, and depth, whether the room is large or small. Each added courtyard and the house of the courtyard, in endless repetition with endless small variations, was a step up in the economic world. Houses were of two courtyards, of three courtyards, of whatever number was desired and needed. And every compound had a wall around it.

The compound where we lived had been bought by the mission from a branch of the Ting family, the principal family of our district, Huang-hsien, the Yellow District. The head of this branch had smoked away in opium his land and then his house. The people of our village, Sung-chia-t'an, the Sung Family Village, and other branches of his family resented his selling to "barbarians" from across the ocean, to the "foreign devils." Even Mr. Chu's diplomacy (Mr. Chu was father's language teacher and a very important person in our lives) when he bargained for the house, and Mr. Ting's need of ready cash could not have made the house ours if it had not been haunted. I wanted very much to see the ghost—a little afraid also, but I never did. Later I was to understand what Mother meant when she said, "The ghost was part of the bargaining." It gave Mr. Ting face to sell.

This compound that had been the home of a Chinese family, that of a wealthy landowner, now housed a whole mission station: church, residence for our family, and guest rooms for visiting church members and traveling missionaries, and a boy's boarding school. Where the Ting family had lived we now lived and where they had worshipped their ancestors we and the Chinese converts now held church services.

3

THE HOUSE OF THE WOMEN

THE CENTER OF OUR living was the House of the Women and the courtyard in front of that house. This was in the middle of the compound as the heart and the stomach are in the middle of the body. Like our skin, the clothes we wear, this third covering, the compound, followed the lines of the body.

When we lived there the courtyard remained the same as when the Ting family had lived there, but the house had been changed to make it more homelike for the American family which was there before ours, at ease only with its own kind of outer covering. These "barbarians" had put in wooden floors over the burnt brick floors. They had changed the windows. The upper half of the whole front, the south wall of the house, above the half wall of burnt brick, had been a serene stretch of lattice, broken only by the door in the center. The had been torn out and the aggressive vertical windows of the West put in instead, two

sashes and twelve panes each. The paper that had covered
the lattice, that had let in the soft light and kept out the
heat and the cold and people's vision, was replaced with
glass, hard and cold, that had to be defended with curtains.
They had taken out the two-leafed Chinese door that hung
on pivots and closed against a high threshold, and put in
a foreign door that swung on hinges. The five *chien* were
still, however, four rooms as they had been when the Ting
family lived there. A wall between two *chien* had been left
out to make a fair-sized living room. Since the roofs were
held up by the pillars, there was no weight on the walls.
These were usually of mud brick and could be put in or
left out at will.

The living room was the center of our family life, but
it was not the center of my life. I never felt comfortable
with the arrangement of the room which I later found to
be an American way to place the furniture. The Chinese
way would have been much more formal. Four pictures
hung on the walls. I liked the two peasants in the re-
production of Millet's *Angelus* that hung on the east wall.
The Old Church, oil painting by Mother herself, was small
and pleasant. I never liked *Pharaoh's Horses* in their
eternal terror. And if I had been naughty, I was sure that
Big Ida's eyes looked accusingly at me. They followed me
around the room. She had been Father's first wife and I
was named for her. Apparently it was the custom in the
hills of North Georgia to name the first daughter of the
second wife after the first. I often wondered if Big Ida
were my guardian angel. Her picture was in the largest
space, on the north wall. That was the place where Chinese hung their ancestral pictures at New Year time, and
they must have wondered, a little, why ours was out all

the time. But to hang an ancestral portrait was, of course, the thing to do.

The round table in the deep corner, with its kerosene lamp, was the center of our evenings when Mother read to us, as we grew older, many of the novels of Dickens and Scott and the tales of Edgar Allen Poe, while she knitted the long black woolen stockings we all wore. How we hated to have her turn the heels, as then she had to count the stitches and stop reading.

There was a cabinet organ against the east wall, to the wailing of which we learned to sing hymns and such songs as "Auld Lang Syne." Shelf of a bookcase, which filled the space between the back door and the dining room wall, became a house, when I took to playing paper dolls and had them visit each other.

John, the brother only eighteen months younger than I, and I learned our alphabet from the blocks our grandmother sent us from America. One day we were sitting playing on the matting from Japan that covered the floor, as it was summer and the doors were all open. I wanted to build houses, and John wanted to build towers. Mr. Chu came through looking for my father. Mr. Chu was a very important person in our lives. He was not only Father's language teacher. He was more than a teacher; he was friend, counselor, and partner in the work of the mission.

"Ha!" he said, coming over to us, "Have you ever seen a block driven through the floor? Would you like to?"

He squatted beside us. All Chinese squat—all classes and at any time. They can squat and rest as long or longer than Americans can sit and rest. And with them it is a graceful posture. Mr. Chu pushed up his long wide sleeve,

long enough to fall below the tips of his fingers, and
picked up a block. Then, with a flourish, he slammed it
on the floor and said, "Go away." His long sleeve fell
over his hand, but this we did not notice. He lifted his
empty hand and pushed back his sleeve. "See. Not even
a trace, not a crack in the floor."

We looked at him in awe. The trick must have been
practiced for the amusement of children on many k'angs,
the wide brick beds of North China, where the family sat
during the day and slept at night. It was a perfect trick
for k'angs and the long wide sleeves.

"Want me to bring it back again?"

We nodded.

"Come back," he commanded, tapping the floor and
passing his hand over the spot where the block had disappeared. "Ah, it is coming," and with a flourish he
brought his hand down on the spot, his sleeve inevitably
falling over his hand, and brought it up again triumphantly
with the block.

It was on the red roses and green moss of the carpet,
which covered the living room floor all winter, that the
mail, which linked us so tenuously with the outer world,
was poured. This was always for us a most dramatic
moment. Every ten days one of the two tall and straight
men from the western part of the province strode through
the Great Back Gate, the Farm Gate, the North Gate of
the compound. He brought the mail he had gone to the
port city of Chefoo to fetch. When I looked at his dark
face with the strong bold features, so different from the
gentler features of the people around me, and his strong
build, I would think of the bandits that lived in the
Western Mountains. I would wonder if he had ever had

to take refuge in the mountains himself. He would rest a night in our compound and then go on to the "exiles" farther west, to the missionaries living in the western part of the province. It took him ten days to walk from Tsinan, the capital of the province Shantung, to Chefoo, the port. At the halfway point he met the other carrier.

The sack of mail for our family was carried into the living room by the cook. That was his right as the most important servant. Father would go to the desk, get the key, unlock the bag, and sort the mail that lay in a pile at our feet, while all stood tensely around. Form was important in the Victorian era. The *Atlantic Monthly*, the *World's Work*, *The Christian Index*, and the weekly edition of the *North China Daily News*, published in Shanghai, were piled up for future reading, but the little envelope from Tallmadge, Ohio, from Grandma Seward (Mother's mother), was pounced upon and read immediately, while the whole family clustered around.

West of the living room was Father's and Mother's bedroom and east was the dining room. Father presided over every meal and insisted that we be prompt. I had been out in the world many years before I could begin a meal comfortably without a blessing first being said.

For breakfast we had a cooked cereal which we called porridge. Some mornings it would be millet, tiny golden grains, still a fragrant memory, other days it would be rice, which I thought dull. Rice in North China was company food. People ate millet, corn, and sorghum seeds with soy beans. Sorghum porridge was a beautiful deep purple. Best of all was cracked wheat, but Mother said it was too much trouble for the cook to make often. The wheat had to be soaked over night, perhaps longer,

and pounded in the deep polished stone mortar (I loved
its black sheen) with a long round stone pestle. They were
part, intact, of the Neolithic Age. Eggs, poached or boiled,
and toast completed the meal. Mother considered fried
eggs unhealthy for us. For dinner we usually had chicken.
How Mother complained! The only meat on the market
was pork. This also was supposed to be unhealthy for us.
Beef we had only in tins from Australia. Cows and oxen
were helpmates in the insistant toil of the farmer. They
could not be killed and eaten. Once a year, in the spring,
there would be mutton, for a brief period. There were
enough Moslems in our district to celebrate their annual
festival. And once a year when the shad ran we had fish
and shad roe. Supper was brief: leftovers.

Beyond the dining room was another bedroom where
we children slept until I was promoted to one of the guest
rooms in the Master's House.

Across the front of the house was a railless veranda.
The roof of tiles, laid one over and one under, swept
down from the ridge pole across the veranda which was
the right width to shut out the sunshine in summer and
let in the long winter rays. This width had been carefully
calculated in ancient times by the Masters of Wind and
Water. That was where Ashley, the baby, slept in his
carriage, and that was where Father and Mother sometimes
sat on warm winter afternoons or summer evenings. On
Saturday afternoons Father would walk up and down, up
and down, working out his sermon for the next day. He
could think better when walking, he said. He walked up
and down other days also: there were always problems to
solve.

The courtyard in front of the house, where the Ting family women had watched their maids wash their clothes and prepare their meals, was where we liked to sit and read and talk: our outdoor living room.

That we lived in the middle houses of the compound, with courtyards and houses in front of us, to the south, with houses and courtyards behind us, to the north, did not seem strange to me. That we were surrounded by two very high walls, was oppressive to my mother, was alien to her. She felt caged, confined. To me, however, the layout and ground plans of the houses when I went to America were difficult to understand. The roofs in America had no dignity and often the rooms were not of harmonious dimensions, the facades were confusing. The pattern for the layout of a Chinese compound, however, was geometric: was made up of straight lines, masses, and open spaces that flowed in rhythmic, harmonious, and repetitive sequences. There was balance in the pattern, both symmetrical and asymmetrical. There was dignity, formality, and privacy. This pattern was the first of which I was conscious in my life. A very satisfying pattern.

The walls also were comforting. Our outer wall was twelve or fifteen feet high, around the whole compound. There was a second wall surrounding the three courtyards and houses where the family lived and the Courtyard and Hall of the Ancestors. This wall was high also but not as high as the outside wall. This also could have been climbed only with a ladder. Between the two walls were the Watchman's Walks. We had no watchman. Father said the mission could not afford one. Anyway there were people in every house except the Hall of the Ancestors and there was nothing to steal. We could hear the watchman in the Ting family house next door. It had been built by a brother of our Mr. Ting, and the two compounds were exactly alike. We could hear the watchman beat out hours, bong bong, on his hollow sounding wood. Also we had the clock, which Father wound every Sunday, to tell us the time.

Mother complained there was no view. She was an American, had been brought up in a house facing the village green. But what did one want with a view when one had flowers in the garden of the Master's Courtyard and in pots to be placed where one pleased; trees in the Women's Courtyard; the slope of the roofs with the rhythmic flow of tiles, one row over and one under; the rhythm of the different roof lines; the sky, each family with its own piece of sky to enjoy?

4

DADA TAKES US OUT
FOR AN AIRING

AFTER DADA HAD MADE the beds and tidied the rooms, it was her duty to take us children out for air and sunshine. Dada was our amah, our nurse, John's and Ashley's and mine. We loved her. John, who had eyes like the sky on a clear day and short sunny curls all over his head, loved her in a somewhat lordly way, for after all she was a woman; and Ashley, who had brown eyes and very little hair on his head, loved her in a possessive way, for he was the baby and claimed most of her attention. She had been my Dada but she was no longer my Dada. She did not pay much attention to me, for I was five years old when I first remember these excursions that went on so many years. I was the oldest and I was a girl.

We would start out from the House of the Women and cross the courtyard going south. On the east side of the walk (paved with burnt brick) that ran across the courtyard to the next house, was a well. In summer we

17

hung the butter and milk in a basket down into the well, so that one was not liquid oil when it came to the table and the other sour before evening. On each side of the walk was a mulberry tree, as there should be in the Court of the Women. The village women came every spring and gathered leaves to feed their silkworms. Huanghsien is not in the silk producing area of China, but many of the housewives raised a few silkworms every year to get a little silk floss for their embroideries, and also because it was traditional for housewives to raise silkworms. The cook made us mulberry pies in the summer before the ground was carpeted with purple berries which the sparrows and the magpies and sometimes the crows enjoyed. Among the family traditions were the blackberry pies of our father's childhood.

"Papa, did you climb the blackberry trees?" I asked, admiring him for his courage and skill. How was I to know that blackberries did not grow on trees when the only berries I had ever seen grew on trees?

The length of the journeys we took was conditioned by Dada's bound feet and the length of our young legs. While she still had to carry Ashley we went to the Court of the Ancestors, and I was content, for I loved that courtyard and the house of that courtyard. It was no small journey at that.

After we crossed the Women's Court we would go up a couple of steps into the hall of the Master's House where Father had his study and where the guest rooms were and where, as I grew older, was my room. On long summer evenings, after being sent to bed, I would watch the rain fall like strings of a bead curtain from the inverted tiles of the roof, or watch the sparrows hopping under the pomegranate tree.

The court of the Master's House was a scholar's garden. From early spring to late autumn something was always in bloom. Peonies lined either side of the brick walk. A bush of tea roses which the Chinese called the *yüeh chi*, the moon season flower, bloomed every month. The pink of the blossoms the Chinese called "powder red" from the powder the women put on their faces. There was a bush of hybiscus by the Second Gate. The pomegranate tree stood in the northwest corner of the court, and August lilies grew luxuriant under the south wall. In autumn the ivy, covering the south wall, would be a blaze of flame and cerise, with little purple shadows, and all winter the lacework of the intertwining vines kept the beauty of the garden alive.

In the middle of the south wall of this courtyard was a formal gate: large double shafts and a roof with spreading wings. This was the Family Gate, the Bride's Gate, and was usually kept closed. This gate was the entrance to the family courtyards from the ancestral part of the compound and was used only on state occasions such as weddings and funerals and the great birthday parties for the elders of the family when the Ting family had lived there. The men of the Ting family came and went by the Little Convenient Gate into the Eastern Watchman's Walk, and we also used this Little Convenient Gate, the *hsiao pien men*.

Stepping through the gate, over the threshold, into the Eastern Watchman's Walk, was always an adventure. I would hold my breath as I looked up and down its

empty sweep. This was the only part of the compound
untouched by our alien life. Men of the past still lived
there where they had practiced archery and held meets
with their friends. I could almost hear the pat of their
soft soled shoes. Their shoes did not clatter and slide on
the brown cobblestones as did the leather ones we sometimes wore. In that instant of crossing the threshold the
walk was mine and theirs—in that instant before the others
came. The long sweep of its length had not been touched.
My eyes would follow the brown cobbled pattern stretching
out before me and the parallel line of the white plastered
wall, coped with grey tiles, above which the tops of the
neighbor's trees billowed against the blue sky, all the way
to the northern end of the walk where the lilac tree grew
against the sunny gable end. The lilac tree was a drift of
snow in spring and a symmetry of green all summer, until
the winter made the bare branches a pattern against the
white wall.

We would turn south, Ashley, the baby, in Dada's
arms, John holding her free hand, and I trudging along
beside her on the other side. She had no hand for me. I
walked on the far side so I could see the walls between
the gable ends of our houses, the gable ends that were
part of the other wall of the walk, and the roofs of the
houses as one after the other they swept up and swept
down. Their grey tiles rippled rhythmically in measured
cadence from one end of the compound to the other.
The Hall of the Ancestors had the highest roof, then came
the Master's House and the Women's House, and then the
House of Those Who Must Also be Cared For, lower than
the others. The roofs then dropped away to those of the
houses in the Farm Courtyard. As I grew older I thought

more about those roofs. They seemed always to be reaching for something. I did not know until I went to Peking that it was the fulfillment of the possibilities within their pattern, a fulfillment I saw in the palaces and temples and homes of that magnificent city.

Three layers of dressed granite, like outsized bricks, made the foundations of each house. Each block was scored with diagonal lines. I knew that the men who drove the chisels which made those diagonal, parallel, and never faltering grooves across the blocks of stone had loved their work, had sung as they worked, had thrown their heads back in arrogance when each block was finished.

At the south end of the walk was the latticed window of the gateman's room. He had nothing to do but tend the gate, see that no intruders came into the compound, and sweep the Entrance Court. The gateman was always some church member who was old and poor and needed a place to live. In old Chinese families he was apt to be a distant and poor relation or an old servant past active duty.

I liked the dignity of the Entrance Court into which we turned from the Watchman's Walk through a gate which was not a moon gate, as in so many great compounds, but was a good gate nevertheless. The Entrance Court was an outdoor entrance hall, leading from the Great Front Gate to all parts of the compound. It was the shoulder of the main compound from which the Eastern and Western Watchman's Walks, like long arms, were around, and guarded the parts of the compound where we lived.

As we came into the court I always looked up at the medallion of carved brick peonies set into the south wall, opposite the Great Gate, and at the pattern made by the square bricks around it. They were set with one corner down and one corner up. This was our Spirit Screen. We did not need a spirit wall built a few feet inside the front gate as in most compounds. The wall between the Entrance Court and the Court of the Ancestors effectively blocked off all evil spirits from coming into the compound. Evil spirits could fly only in straight lines. Also, and more practically, the spirit screen inside a gate blocked off all vision, from the street, of the family living quarters.

That all the gates in all the courts, and all the doors, except the Great Front Gate, were on a central axis, did not seem strange to me. Had all the gates to all the courtyards and all the doors to all the houses been opened at the same time we could have seen through the compound from the Entrance Court to the Threshing Floor outside the Great Back Gate and to the Wall beyond the Threshing Floor. The Great Front Gate, however, was east of the central axis. When I was older and began to ask questions, the answers were not much help. "Only an emperor can bear the power, stand the effects, of a Great Front Gate on the Central Axis." That I saw when I went to Peking and saw the Great Front Gate of the city in line with all the main gates of the Forbidden City, the Imperial Palace. All the powers of the air would have been able to sweep through our compound had the Great Front Gate been in the center of the front wall. The front gates of all families other than the imperial, they told me, should be to the east or to the west, preferably to the east. When

I continued to press for a reason and to ask why, none knew the reason, only that it was so. When I continued to question, the answer came, "A man turns his face to the east." When in Peking I found a book and lost it, a book that described Peking city in anthropomorphic terms. The limbs, the sense organs, the vital organs were all assigned to parts of the city. Ch'ien Men, the Great Front Gate of the city was, naturally, the head of the man, Peking—No Cha. Being imperial, he turned his head neither to the east nor to the west but held it high and looked straight forward. Naturally the city faced south. In later years in Mongolia, I found that all the tents faced, as the people said, south, but they were always a bit to the east of south. It is logical also that the main gate from the street should be to one side so strangers walking by could not see into the family courts or even into the Court of the Ancestors, even if there were no curtain walls.

The House of the Entrance Court was the one house in the compound that faced north since it backed onto the street. The house was used, therefore, as basements and attics are used in other countries, for servants' quarters, offices, and storage. The gateman lived in the *chien* at the eastern end by the Great Front Gate. The Great Front Gate itself, the Gate Cave, as the Chinese called the space it occupied, was a whole *chien*, without front and back walls, and was bisected by the two huge leaves of the gate. In the two *chien* at the eastern end had lived the Ting family steward, and lived our young cook, after the school had opened in the Farm Courtyard and sent all who had lived in its many rooms to other quarters. There was also the three-*chien* reception room, where the Master of the house could meet his business associates and any men he could not take into the family courts. These rooms had been made into a carpenter's shop where Sa Shih-fu made Grand Rapids furniture (from pictures) for the homesick missionaries who did not know the beautiful Chinese furniture.

As we passed through the Entrance Court I would tug at Dada's coat—that blue cotton coat that came to her knees—and say, "I want to see Sa Shih-fu." I always wanted to find the perfect curl from among those he pared off the boards he was planing, as he sat straddled on the bench and pushed the plane away from him, but never did. Sometimes if it were chilly and we could not spend a long time outdoors, Dada would take us in to visit him for awhile. As we passed his door we could almost always hear him singing the little song that seemed to have no end, the little song the artisans sang as they worked.

During those early years the steward's quarters were not used, but the young cook moved there when I was eight or nine. These rooms are as clear in my mind as though I saw them yesterday. No rooms except those of the abbot in a great Peking temple, or of a scholar in an upper room in Shanghai, had so definite a spirit, so perfect entity.

Chao Te-shan, the name by which we knew the young cook, his school name, was not the name I knew him by many years later when he was a retired mandarin in Peking. Every added dignity meant a new name, given by admiring friends. These rooms, however, I always associated in my mind with this amazing person. I do not remember him as the teen-age country boy brought from the poverty area of P'ingtu, where people ate sweet potatoes and not much else the year 'round, brought to tend our cow. That was when I was too young to notice. And I do not remember him haunting the kitchen, that sitting room for the servants, where he watched the old cook to such good ends that, when the old cook retired to become a farmer, Chao Te-shan asked Mother for the job.

While he was cook he would spend all his spare time in the school rooms, sitting humbly in the back and learning what the little boys were learning. He dogged Mother's steps with his notebooks, getting her to correct his English exercises. He learned English so well that he became interpreter to the American consul in Chefoo. With the knowledge gained in his correspondence courses from Purdue University and the friends and contacts he made while interpreter, he planned and organized the building of the first motor road across East Shantung. This was from Chefoo, the port, to Weihsien, on the railroad the Germans were building. With the money he made from the building of this road he went to Peking to live as a retired mandarin. Many mandarins, officials, chose Peking as the place to which to retire.

In Peking, when I met him, in the home of my friend, the retired mandarin Wu Yung, whose story about the flight of the Empress Dowager I translated, he did not bring up old times. Nor did I. He did not bury the past from pride of present position, I was sure, but because his latest dealings with missionaries had not been pleasant and in his mind he probably still connected me with that compound in Huang District, although I had left it and the ways of its people far behind, as he had.

I could not understand why the missionaries thought it necessary to throw him out of the church. Perhaps because I was brought up in a Chinese house, with Chinese people all around me, I have never been able to think there was only one way to do anything. I could never understand why the missionaries were so adamant against the Chinese marriage system. It suited the ways of the times. These have now been changed to suit the new ways. Even in the old days most men had only one wife. Most men wanted only one. Few could afford more. Many could never get together the money needed to set up a home and have even one wife. The wife's duties, in those days, were more to the Old Home and to the mother-in-law than to the husband. Chao Te-shan's mother had no daughter. She took a small famine waif into her home as the wife-to-be for her teenage son and as someone to help her with the housework. In due time she and Chao Te-shan were married and the young wife had a son. She was a good woman, a filial woman, a very dull woman. Chao Te-shan built a fine compound for his mother and wife, whom, as was the right thing to do, he left with his mother and son in the Old Home, and took for himself in Peking a wife of his own choice. The missionaries, outraged, insisted he be expelled from the church. Chao Te-shan promptly built his own church in Peking and gathered his own congregation. My friend Wu Yung and his family were among the members of this church even though Wu Yung had his own Buddhist shrine in his home, in his library, where he spent much time copying out the Buddhist sutras. Why should not one take the good of all religions, all striving upward toward the light?

Over the years I can still feel the atmosphere, feel the richness of thought in that room where Chao Te-shan had lived and see the four paintings on the wall. Marketing and cooking for us, studying English and the Chinese classics in the school, he still had time to take painting lessons. The neat pile of books, each covered with blue cloth to protect it from the dust (probably done by himself), the scholars ink slab and little water container, and the blue and white china holder with its "forest of pens," capped brushes standing erect, was more of a scholar's study than the rooms of any of the teachers in the school.

Also, I learned, as the years went by, that Chao Te-shan was a good man. He had carried out one of the main principles of the way of life of that great civilization, at that time the pattern of the land. I have phrased this principle to myself: "Every privilege has its corresponding responsibility and every responsibility its corresponding privilege." The middle generation, the man in his earning years, had the responsibility of caring for those above him who once had cared for him, of caring for his parents (and uncles and aunts and grandparents, if any) and for those below him, his wife and children, and nephews and nieces and any that needed him in that generation. Endlessly the generations moved forward: the cared for became the caring, until the second time for being cared for arrived. Chao Te-shan carried out his responsibilities toward the mother who had cared for him and for his wife by providing a fine compound for them and money to live well, and by giving his son the best education available. It was then his privilege to arrange for himself the life he wanted to live. In his religious life he followed the same pattern. He fulfilled his responsibility to the old home church by generous, very generous, donations as long as he had the privilege of the fellowship. When that was withdrawn, he carried out the responsibility to his religion by founding his own church and had the privilege of worship as he thought worship should be.

I do not know who lived in those rooms after Chao Te-shan left. Probably one of the teachers in the school.

5

THE HALL OF THE ANCESTORS

T HE SECOND GATE WAS the most important gate. It was not as large or as grand as the Great Front Gate. It did not have a gate cave, a whole *chien* to itself, but it had its own roof, high above the walls. In some compounds the Second Gate was the Woman's Gate or the Family Gate, but in our compound it was the gate into the Ancestral Courtyard. Our Second Gate was famous as one of the most beautiful in the Huang district. The brackets that held up the heavy, wide-spreading tiled roof were sturdy and simple, the finials for the cross beams well carved.

To walk up the wide shallow steps to the gate and cross the high threshold was to perform a ritual of great dignity. The men of the Ting family must have walked up those stone steps clothed in their ceremonial robes on high occasions. Even the church members, poor farmers and artisans for the most part, and the servants and teachers in our families, walked up those steps and through that gate with added dignity. One day I saw the son of Mrs. Chang of Hou Pai Lung Chang Chia (the Chang family of the Rear White Dragon Village) walk up those steps and I saw a thing I had never seen before. I saw the steps mounted as they should be mounted, saw the ritual performed, and the picture is vivid in my memory.

Young Mr. Chang was about twenty years old. He was not handsome, but he was very elegant. His black hair was oiled and hung down his back in a thick braid, so thick it certainly was not all his own. The braiding started far enough away from his head for daring and to give him style, and yet not far enough away to be considered dissolute. His long silk gown, belted in at the waist with a silk sash, hung down in a box pleat behind. His little sleeveless over-jacket was of a new cut I never before had seen. His shoulders drooped as an elegant scholar's shoulders should droop, though I never heard of his being noted for his scholarship. In fact, his skill with the dice, or lack of it, was all I ever heard of any skill of his.

Elegantly he swayed across the Entrance Court, raised his head and looked at the tiles flowing down the roof of the gate, and let his head droop between his shoulders. From side to side he swayed, thrusting his feet to the right and to the left. It was the elegant scholar's walk. I wondered if he always took time to walk that way. His every movement as he drooped and swayed up the wide shallow steps proclaimed he knew he was entering the most important part of the compound and that he was doing it the right way. He was the only one I ever saw to give the gate its ritual due and I saw him only this once.

The Courtyard of the Hall of the Ancestors was paved with brick and little white pebbles the size of hazel nuts. The bricks were laid in a modified Greek key pattern which the Chinese call the turning pattern, the *wan tzu* pattern. There is also a play on words. As the pattern goes on and on, it could be called the pattern of the word 'everlasting'. The white pebbles filled in the pattern made by the bricks.

I always tried, walking from the Second Gate across the Courtyard of the Ancestors to the porch across the front of the Ancestral Hall, to stay on the bricks only and not to let my feet cross the seams between the bricks or touch the pebbles. This was not easy, for the bricks were small and the pattern turned and turned on itself. I did not know (I had not the key), I did not know that I was dancing, trying to dance, the three-or four-thousand-year-old ritual dance of death and life again, the fertility dance of death and rebirth, danced before the ancestors. This old dance of the maidens, hand-linked, two steps forward and one step back, weaving between the upright posts of fertility, of life, of the ancestors (later stylized into tablets) had become, in the centuries, forgotten by the people around me. But it was symbolized by the bricks laid in the pavement of the court before the Ancestral Hall, weaving endlessly around the bright white pebbles; and has persisted in the seedling dance of the people at their festivals, in the *yang-ko* dance.

Dada would carry Ashley across the court to the railless veranda and sit against one of the black pillars that held up the roof, and take out the darning she carried always with her. Sometimes I would stop to look at the tiles rippling down the roof, one grey row over and one

grey row under, and at the rhythm of the latticed doors
and windows that flowed across the front of the hall,
across the width of the court. If I heard the pigeons I
would run up on the veranda to see if I could spot their
nests back under the eaves. I could see the birds strutting
on the beams and the piles of their droppings that Mother
complained about so much. I could not understand why.
I did not mind the acrid odor. I never saw any nests and
would avoid the court the days Mother gave orders for
them to be destroyed. That this was ever really done, I
doubt. There seemed always to be the same number of
pigeons. They are a favorite bird with the Chinese. I
think the gateman raised a dust and swept out some of the
loose straw.

In the spring, when the fragrant grasses that grew
between the pebbles were fresh and young, we would
pluck them for Dada and she would braid little baskets
and grasshoppers and tigers for us. If she did not feel
too thronged with the mending, she would even play with
us. She would stand Ashley in front of her trousered
knees and, holding his hands, rock back and forth the
way the carpenters pulled back and forth when they sawed
the great trunks of trees to make us boards, one man on
the ground and one on a scaffold to give the strong up
and down pull. Dada would chant:

Tzu ke ke chu	Tzu ke, the saw cuts
Ke lao-niang lao huai shu	Cuts down Grandmother's
	old locust tree

Sometimes we could get her to chant with us:

Hsiao lao shu	The little mouse
Shang teng t'ai	Climbed onto the lamp-stand
Tou yu ch'ih	Stealing oil to eat
Hsia pu lai	Couldn't get down again
Chi chi, wa wa	Chi chi, wa wa
Chiao nai-nai	Calling his grandmother
Chiu-tzu hsiao wei-pa	Who seized him by his tail
La hsia-lai	And pulled him down

I did not wonder why the grandmother, *nai-nai*, who pulled the little mouse down by his tail, was his paternal grandmother (of course he lived with her as it should be) or why the grandmother, *lao-niang*, who lost her locust tree, was the maternal one.

I don't think that Dada thought the rhyme I learned from the other little girls was proper:

Pa Kou Pa, ta men lien	Bark dog bark, lift the door curtain
An chia yu ke hao mei jen	In our house there's a beautiful person
Chan tsui pa, hung tsui ts'un	Her chin is pointed, her lips are red
Shuo ch'u hua, hsiao ssu jen	When she speaks you laugh yourself to death

John and I would skip off to finish our game of "Not step into the river," or to climb the trees, as we called the shrubs in the rockeries. On the east and on the west, built against the walls of the Ancestral Courtyard, were two raised beds with beveled brick retaining walls. Evergreens for the ancestors grew in them: boxwood on the east and spiney dwarf cedars on the west. We liked the boxwood better. The centers had been cut away so each shrub was a bowl in which we could sit. The shrubberies were useful in our games of hide and seek when the Chu children came to play with us.

Mother took pictures of her friends in front of the boxwood terrace. That was the spot they always chose as the background for their photographs. They would set a table with a vase of flowers on it or a clock and a chair beside it in front of the terrace and then pose. When I was grown and saw the paintings of scholars in their formal gardens, the conversation pieces, I understood. Among Mother's friends who had their pictures taken were the Lan family. Mr. and Mrs. Lan looked so much alike they could have been brother and sister. They were first cousins. That a girl should follow her father's sister in marriage, enter the same family, was considered good. An aunt was more likely to be a good mother-in-law than one not related, was the reason given. First cousins of the same surname were considered brothers and sisters, and marriage between them impossible; it would have been incestuous. Mrs. Lan's father was her husband's mother's brother. They lived in our village and they had twins. I loved those twins and called them my little sisters. They were my little "sworn sisters." One was right-handed and one was left-handed. When they ate, their chins reached only to the edge of the table, and the long North China chopsticks, which seemed almost as long as they were tall, stuck out above their heads, one pair to the right and one pair to the left. Mother took our pictures with one of the twins standing on each side of me in front of the boxwood terrace. I was also dressed in Chinese clothes. That was my favorite picture for a long time. The mother of the twins and their older sister hid my cropped hair with a Chinese band-hat and placed a flower over each ear where the braids should have been. They thought that people should look as attractive as possible, especially when they were having their pictures takes.

It was to this formal terrace that I ran alone the day Mother left for P'eng-lai to see the doctor about her running ear. P'eng-lai was almost a day's journey (60 *li* = 20 miles) by mule-litter away, and Mother would be gone many days. This was the first time Mother had ever gone away and not taken us with her. I decided that, as a filial daughter, I must weep because she was gone. I took my little white wooden stool (a new one Mother had just given me) and placed it in front of the terrace and sat down to weep. But the tears would not come. My handkerchief, held to my face, remained dry. I stuck out my tongue and wet a spot, but it did not look as though it had been made by tears. It would not fool anyone. It did not fool me. Whom, anyway, did I want to fool? Not even myself. Why should I pretend? Suddenly I realized it did not matter whether Mother went to P'eng-lai without me or not. She would be back in a few days and Father and Dada were with us. I put my handkerchief in my pocket and ran away to play.

There was another reason I liked to play best on the side of the courtyard with the boxwood. That side had not been mutilated. Inside the Ancestral Hall, which was now used as the mission's church, was another mutilation. A curtain had been put up to separate the men from the women, so the women could come to church and yet not

be seen by the men, by strange men other than those of
their own families. Putting up a curtain, ugly as it was,
did not spoil the hall. A curtain could be hung and taken
away again. It did not destroy the structure, the pattern.
It was temporary like a piece of paper blowing, a temporary mutilation. But in the southeast corner of the
court, between the western terrace and the south wall,
they had dug a hole. I did not like to look at that hole.
Even the thought of it hurt me—hurt as though it were
my flesh that had been cut into—that the pattern of the
courtyard and of the bricks and the pebbles had been
disturbed and broken.

The hole was a baptistry. They had lined it with
white plaster that was always scaling off. When dry the
hole was ugly and gaping. When anyone had been accepted
by the church members into the church, and was to be
baptised, the hole was filled with water. I would watch
the men carrying load after load of water—a pail on each
end of their carrying poles—and pouring it with a swish
into the hole. Since to work on Sunday was considered
wrong, and the baptisms had to be on Sunday when all
came to church, and since the water ran out rather quickly
through the plaster and bricks of the walls, the water had
to be put in on Saturday afternoon and the baptistry
filled to the top. By church time it would be between the
waist line and the chest level for a grown-up. On Sunday
at church time Father, as pastor of the church, would go
down the brick steps into the water and stand there.
Then the new church member, led to the brink by the
deacons, would go down the brick steps into the water
and face Father. When Father had said a few words about
the meaning of the ceremony and made a short prayer,

he would take the new member by the shoulders and dip him under the water. The new church member would come up looking drowned and unpleasant, though he had been under but a moment.

To the new church member it was initiation into the club. There are always rites at initiations. It took me a long time to realize that the people thought of the church as a club. The Chinese word chosen by the early missionaries was *hui*, "club, organization, assembly." The Baptists were the Chin Hsin Hui, the "Club of the Immersed Believers," and the Presbyterians were the Chang Lao Hui, the "Club of the Elders." The churches in general were *chiao hui*, "clubs of the doctrine," whichever one was preached, or assemblies of the religion, *chiao* being a doctrine or religion. In old China there were no religious organizations in the pattern of Western religious denominations or churches, with organized congregations that gathered in bodies at stated periods for worship. Their religion was either a family matter, the ancestor worship, and the rites were performed at home; or an individual matter, where the person went to whatever temple he wished and worshipped individually at whatever shrine he chose. A temple was not built by congregation but by a pious individual who might pay for it himself or spend a lifetime soliciting enough funds to get one built. The nearest analogy to church membership was the trade guild and the secret society. These had their headquarters, usually, in temples, in quarters hired from the temples. The secret societies had a more varied membership than the trade guilds, and were, perhaps, except for the secrecy, a better analogy to churches. These were all clubs or assemblies. One of the most noted of the secret societies was the *Ke Lao Hui*, the "Society of the Elder Brothers." The missionaries eventually brought in a new meaning to the old word, and *hui* became known also as denomination. I had been taught, however, that church was a place where God was worshipped as in a temple. Some of the new members undoubtedly saw the baptism ceremony as Father saw it, a symbol of the death of the old sinful way of life and the resurrection into the love of God, and also a symbolic washing away of sin. Father's face would be beautiful as he raised a new member, symbolically, from death to life.

To me, however, it was a grotesque and somewhat indecent ceremony, performed in a pit that had broken the harmony of the court, that had scarred the court, that had cut into the living pattern, into the living body of the compound that was something more than a compound.

Why did I feel that way? How do I know? I do not remember ever talking about it to anyone. I do not remember hearing anyone talking about it. I probably felt it from the feelings and thoughts of the people around me, from Dada's feelings, perhaps, and the feelings of others who stood around that gaping hole, and from a word here and a glance there.

There was another mutilation. There was a blind hole in the south wall, a niche that was empty. The wide sweep of a blank wall is beautiful, but there is always something wrong about a place prepared and not occupied. The niche was built of dressed brick, lined with it, and over it was a little carved brick roof. But it was empty. I did not know what should have been there until years later. There are questions one does not ask. There are

questions one does not think of asking. There should have
been a tablet to Heaven and Earth in that niche.

If Ta Pao and Ching-tzu, the older Chu children, the
son and daughter of Father's teacher, could get away from
their many duties and come to play with us, we were
happy indeed. Then John, who spent more and more time
with the men servants and, after Mother had started her
school, with the school boys, would come also and play
with us in the Court of the Ancestors and in the Hall. We
would play blind-man's buff and hide-and-seek in and out
of the shadows and across the great shafts of light that
came through the narrow high open doors, slanting blocks
of light, shafts of light in which a million fairies danced.
One day I slipped and fell on the hard polished brick floor
and raised a lump on my head. Ta Pao rubbed my head
and comforted me.

More and more each year I loved the Hall of the
Ancestors. It was beautiful. I could shut my eyes to the
trumpery curtain between the men and the women. I
could shut my eyes to the rows and rows of ugly and
uncomfortable benches and look instead at the open rafters, lacquered yellow-brown, with the square fine-textured,
flat grey bricks above them. I could look at the polished
heavy beams, great logs of wood stretched from pillar to
pillar across the hall, and my eyes could soar with the
brackets that built up to the ridge pole, holding the weight
of the roof. I could look at the huge polished bricks, two
feet square, that paved the floor, and resent the benches
that desecrated them. I could look at the pattern made
by the sun coming through the paper on the lattice work
of the windows and the doors across the whole front of
the hall, and watch the tiny golden specks dancing in the

shafts of light cutting across the hall from the tall open
doors, reaching from cross-beam to floor, shafts cut out
of darkness, cut by a giant hand and thrust into the room.

On Sundays there were people sitting on the benches,
the ugly stiff benches with backs that cut everyone in the
wrong places. The women, among whom I sat, were for
the most part dull housewives, the current babies nursing
at their breasts or sleeping wrapped in the safe nests of
their mothers' wide coats. At any moment in the service
one of the harried mothers might be running around the
benches after a two-, three- or four-year-old not yet come
to the age of reason which comes, the Chinese say, at the
age of seven (six in Western count), and therefore impossible to keep still. There was, however, the eldest daughter
of the Lan family. Tiny bells tinkled at the end of the
silver chain that held on her hat, that band of black satin
across her forehead on which were sewn so many pretty
pieces of jade and silver. She wore her shining black hair
in a pleated knot lower on her neck than the local women
wore their coiled knots. "Shanghai style," I heard them
mutter to each other. She had a little face with a pointed
chin and very bright black eyes. Though her feet had
been unbound when her parents joined the church, she
still walked with the "graceful swaying" motion of the
women with bound feet. I knew that the people around
me thought her attractive and "too daring."

If I sat on the end of the front bench, near the
doors, I could see the men crossing the court to their
side of the hall. There were stolid farmers and small
shopkeepers, the servants of the mission, the teachers and
students of the school, and Dr. Fan. It was a good day
when I saw Dr. Fan's green-yellow velvet topcoat crossing

the court. It came to his knees, and he wore it over a purple robe that came to just above his ankles, very full and tied with a sash. I could see the ends from under the short topcoat. I would look for the smile wrinkles crinkling around his nearsighted eyes. He had a long sparse beard to show his dignity as a scholar and a doctor and dispenser of drugs, even though as yet he had no grandson of his own name.

The other men all wore the usual indigo-blue dyed gowns and trousers, with an occasional half length topcoat of black. But the clothes dyed in indigo, depending on the number of times they had been washed, would be all shades of blue from deep midnight to the gay shades of the cornflower and even the blue of the midday sky.

As I sat on the bench and watched the church fill, I could smell the earthy smell of the congregation, like the smell of healthy small boys. In the spring it was laced with garlic and chives and fresh onions. They were earth smells, good smells. There was always the knowledge of the indigo of their clothes and sometimes a whiff of sandalwood from a holiday garment not often worn.

I never learned to shut out the noise the congregation made as they tried to sing hymns, as they dragged, slurred, and flattened, struggling with the alien scales and cadences. They did not do so badly with Father's favorite hymn and I would join my small piping to the roll of "How firm a foundation, ye saints of the Lord/Is laid for your faith in His excellent Word." Even then, before I had rejected the symbolism, I disliked the wail of "There is a fountain filled with blood/Drawn from Emmanuel's veins." As often as I thought it would be granted, I asked Mother, who played the little cabinet organ, for the hymn some

missionary with imagination and musical ability had set
to an old Buddhist chant. The deep Chinese chest tones
then came out, and the invocation to deity rolled out as
it should, in the pentatonic scale.

Once a month, before the last hymn, Father would
announce that the communion service would follow the
hymn, and those who were not church members might
leave as the hymn was sung. Mother had opened a bottle
or two of the grape juice she had put up the summer
before, and the cook had baked the thin unleavened cakes,
which, marked before they were baked, Mother broke
into small squares. All right and proper for church members to have their special meal. Did not clan members
meet at their temple for annual dinners? Did not the
guild members have meals together? I wonder the church
members did not think the repast skimpy. The symbolism
was explained to the congregation each time, of course,
and did not shock them. Legends there were of ancient
times when sons were required to drink the broth of their
father's bones.

When I was somewhat older, I was shocked one communion Sunday to see the new teacher in the school, a
young man from the newly established Presbyterian college
in P'eng-lai, later moved to Weihsien, walk out with the
"heathen." I thought him very handsome. His long black
queue was very black and very thick and very shiny. The
rich blood showed through the ivory-colored skin of his
face. As it was summer he wore a long, white grass linen
gown. That he should walk out of the communion service
caused my first rebellion against organized religion and
started my first piece of research.

As soon as we were back home I went into the attack.

"Why did Mr. Liu walk out? Is he not a Christian?"

"Yes, but he is a Presbyterian."

"But are not Presbyterians Christians?"

"Yes, but he had not been baptised, immersed, the way Jesus was. The Presbyterians sprinkle."

I got out the family Bible, looked through the concordance, and read every verse that referred to baptism. Nowhere did I find a command to dip people under water.

This was my first encounter with Fundamentalism (my parents' brand was quite mild in general). Exclusiveness in religion did not seem Christian to me. I must also have been thinking Chinese thoughts again. Each person believed what he wished to believe, and worshipped in whatever temple he wished, and had whatever shrine he wished in the home, whether other members of the family worshipped there or not. Ancestor worship was the only worship performed in groups, and those were generation by generation, and in the family.

All through the sermon I would sit bored, though in time I came to respect father for the very thing that bored me then. He never preached a really long sermon, but half an hour or even twenty minutes is long to a child, and he always preached about the same thing, whatever text he took. He never told dramatic stories about hellfire, as did many of the other missionaries, or tell about Daniel in the lion's den or Shadrak, Meshak, and Abednego in the fiery furnace; nor did he thunder hair-raising rebukes. Always he was telling about the love of God and of Jesus, His Son, and of the Brotherhood of all Mankind.

Father would stand on the low platform, just high enough for his head and shoulders to appear above the curtain, so the women could see him and listen to what he said. He very seldom turned his head to look at them. He looked at the men in front of him.

The platform where father stood to preach was where the ancestral shrine and the long table of offerings had stood when the church had been the Ting family Ancestral Hall. The table in front of him, where the Bible lay, was where the mat had lain on which the members of the Ting family knelt to kowtow in worship to their ancestors. The rest of the hall would then have been empty but for the pillars—empty, bare, and beautiful-empty so people could stand and kneel and make patterns in their standing and kneeling, as they knelt one after the other before the tablets of their ancestors.

6

THE HOUSE OF THOSE WHO
MUST ALSO BE CARED FOR

WE COULD PLAY IN the courtyard back of the House of the Women, for this courtyard and the house of the courtyard where the extra uncles and aunts and cousins the Ting family had lived, was now our kitchen court. The kitchen and store room were in the little house against the east wall. Mother, homesick for the vegetables she had known, had made the west side of the courtyard into a garden where she planted peas and lima beans and sweet corn. She even tried an asparagus bed. Chinese vegetables in their almost endless variety she never knew. The ones she used were, to her, substitutes only. She planted sweet peas for beauty.

This was the courtyard to which the boxes from Montgomery Ward were brought each summer. Many early winter evenings were spent poring over the Montgomery Ward catalogues and making out the order that would bring these boxes, six months later, to this court-

45

yard, after a journey by rail across the United States, by ocean liner to Shanghai, by coastal steamer to Chefoo, by Chinese junk to the little fishing village eighteen li (six miles) from us, and by mule cart to our home.

All of us gathered around the boxes as Father opened them, drew out the long shiny steel nails that the cook so carefully gathered and took away for what use I never knew. Chinese nails, at that time, were hammered out of iron and were used more as bolts are used than modern nails. Houses and furniture were made without nails, beautifully fitted together. The strong shining American nails were highly prized. I almost held my breath as the parcels came out one after another. One year there was a doll for me. I did not care for that doll. It had a shiny porcelain head and stiff stuffed body. It was a dead thing. There were books, a whole set of Dickens one year and Scott another.

Nostalgic Mother always ordered a half gallon of clover honey she had been used to as a child. Chinese raised bees and collected honey. They did not strain it, however, but melted the comb into the honey and sold it in the medicine shops. Mother's honey, therefore, never lasted as long as she had hoped. Before the day had passed the procession of village women began. The boy or Dada would come into the dining room, while we were eating, or into the sitting room, while Mother was reading to us, and hold out a little blue and white bowl. "She is waiting outside. Her mother-in-law, . . ." or it might be her son, or her husband—her old mate—who was ill, very ill, "has suffered the wind"—had a cold. Mother did not need to hear the end of the sentence. She would nod her head and a bit of the precious foreign honey, believed to be

more potent than the Chinese honey (and in what country
are not imported goods considered superior?), would be
taken away. More potent or not, it was certainly more
accessible and certainly cheap, as they got it for nothing.
The village women would take their portions home,
heat the honey in wine (more like very strong vodka)
and give it to the patient to drink. The patient would
already be in the thick quilt cocoon, on the warm k'ang,
waiting for the healing sweat. Enough honey would
be left to us for a few waffle breakfasts and a few meals
with honey and hot biscuits—a special concession to
Father's Southern taste.

Honey was not the only drug Dada or the cook would
ask for as spokesmen for the village people. In the dining
room was a wall cupboard filled with bottles. This was
Mother's dispensary. The village women trusted foreign
drugs for sores on their skins that came from the dry
climate, the blowing dust, and lack of soap. Soap, introduced by the "Ocean People," foreigners, those from
across the seas, was one of the most prized of gifts at
that time, rare and imported as it was. The cleaning
agents the people used, lye and soda, were harsh to the
skin. Mother's ointments were welcomed. Gradually they
also took her worm medicines and accepted her eye drops.
Some of them brought their babies to be vaccinated when,
once a year, we and the school boys (in the school Mother
ran) were vaccinated from the little glass tubes that came
from Shanghai. So many of the older people were pock-
marked that no one thought it strange to see pock-marks
or wonder at the many babies with pustule-covered faces.
They were getting well, the trouble had come out and
not gone inward and killed them. Vaccination was new

in our provincial area, but it was making its way in the minds of these very practical people.

Some people, though not many, even came to Mother for that most common of their ills, the pain in the "heart-hollow." They had learned there were foreign drugs that soothed even that gnawing distress without the danger of contracting the opium habit. Most of them, however, trusted more in their plasters, rounds of black paste between squares of oiled paper. Carved in wood, they were the signs hung outside the medicine shops to tell those who could not read that drugs were sold within. There were big plasters to go over the stomach or back, sizes suitable for each part of the body, or any ache. We could see women and sometimes men, with a little plaster on each temple, from where most easily the healing virtues could get through to the head that was aching. Often instead of plasters the pulling treatment, or cupping, was used. Sometimes Dada would come in the morning with the three round marks on her forehead, where the skin was darker and the flesh raised. Then we knew she had had the three small cups, with burning paper in them, clamped to the skin. Sometimes instead of burning paper artemesia would be used. Sometimes she would have three red lines down her throat where the strong fingers of an old wise woman had plucked. They always said that the illness had started with an anger. "I was angry and the fire burned in me." Most illnesses started with an anger and the fire in them that the anger kindled.

Another common diagnosis we did not hear as often because not many people traveled widely. Even across the range of hills that ran down the center of the province, or even into the next *hsien*, the next county, the soil and water might be different. *"Pu fu shui t'u* (The soil and water do not agree with him)," was a well-known diagnosis. Only the soil and water of one's own native place could really agree with one, though with time one could get accustomed to the new. Officials traveling to other provinces were known to carry parcels of their own home earth with them.

Often Mother was called upon to do that which she had no power to do: Save a life. It would be a young daughter-in-law's brother seeking to save his sister's life because he loved her and because it was his lifelong duty to protect her and her children. Or it would be a member of her husband's family seeking to save his family's face and fortune—the fortune however large or small—that might all go in lawsuits should she die, should she succeed in taking this ultimate revenge on the mother-in-law who had so harried her. "She has swallowed mercury." Households bought mercury to kill lice and nits. Mother learned the antidote to mercury poisoning the next time she saw a doctor, and the next box from Montgomery Ward had a book on poisons and their antidotes.

Already there was a *Complete Family Doctor* on the top shelf of the medicine chest. John and I would get it down sometimes and look at the pictures of the skeletons and the layers of cut-outs attached to either side to show how the skeleton was covered. That the genitals were left out seemed strange to us.

"She has eaten matches." The desperate young woman would soak a box of matches and drink the water. For a young daughter-in-law to get hold of poison was not easy. "She stole some of her father-in-law's opium and drank it." Not every father-in-law had opium, nor was it always where the desperate daughter-in-law could get it.

Sometimes they did not come for help, but the news would drift in. "She jumped down a well." So many unhappy young daughters-in-law jumped down wells that became customary for a bride's brother to walk by her red-covered sedan chair as she was taken to the new home she had never seen. His duty was to hold up a red embroidered scarf between her chair and any well or pool of water or temple as they passed. This was to ward off any spirit of a suicide who might be lurking at the place where its body had died or, as in a temple, a place where spirits were tolerated. These spirits were bound, the people believed, to these places until other suicides took their places and set them free. There was therefore ever the danger to any passers-by of being urged against their will to do away with themselves. Young brides did not need too much persuasion. Always the comment was, "Her destiny was a bitter one. She did not draw (from life's lottery) a good mother-in-law."

The men had bitter destinies also. The word debt was always in their mouths. Our mother, who had taught school for years in California to pay off her father's debts, had taught us it was wrong to go into debt, but neither Father nor Mother seemed ever to blame these people. It was as though their debts were like the pockmarks on their faces, were things they could not help. Every year those that emigrated to Manchuria were many. *Shang Kuan tung* (gone east of the pass—into Manchuria) was a household phrase.

I was too young to understand what Father and Mother meant when they said, "Spent too much on the grandfather's funeral," or "The rains washed away his crop." Filial piety demanded a suitably magnificent funeral, and a man must feed his family. Who had grain for the spring planting? Who had money to lend but the landlord? What did I know about loan sharks and usury? Compounded every month at anything from ten to fifty percent.

Many of the taxes they had to pay seemed unfair. An official got what he could out of the people and sent what he must to those above. The person most often cursed was the *yayi*, the yamen runner, the messenger from the official headquarters, the one official, and a very small one, with whom the people came into contact. His duty was to collect taxes. *Yayi* came to occupy the same section of my mind as devil.

These debts gave the men real trouble, perhaps a lifetime of bitter trouble. It bit into their faces until the pockmarks disappeared into the lines and seams and darkened their children's faces with insufficient nourishment.

There was nothing in Mother's medicine chest to help these people. Nothing she could send for to Montgomery Ward. The best she could do was to bring as many of their sons as she could into her school and teach them English and arithmetic so they could go out and earn money for their families. It was not strange, therefore, that the House of Those Who Must Also be Cared For should become dormitories for the boys' school Mother started.

I liked these rooms. The *k'angs*, the mud-brick platforms, through which ran flues to heat them, on which the aunts and the cousins had sat by day and slept at night, had not been taken out when the missionaries took over the compound. The floors were still of laid-burnt brick. These rooms had been used, before the school was organized, for church members when they stayed over-night. Sometimes John, Ashley, and I slept there with Dada when Mother went away a few days. Sometimes we played tea-party, sitting on either side of a little low table on the *k'ang*, sat with our legs folded under us as had the people who had sat there in the past.

7

THE BACK OF THE COMPOUND

BEHIND THE HOUSE OF Those Who Must Also be Cared For, between it and the Farm Courtyard, was the northern stretch of the Watchman's Walk. It joined together the Eastern and Western Watchman's Walks: like the clasped hands of the two long arms stretching around us and protecting us.

The Western Watchman's Walk was the service walk. There were little convenient gates from it into the courts where we lived. It was half covered over for storage, and there were little rooms built along it under the half roof. One was the store room for coal, and one was the family privy. All along the walk were the boxes and storage jars, the lumber being seasoned, anything a large compound would need but did not want in the courtyards and the houses.

Near the Little Convenient Gate from the Court of Those Who Must Also be Cared For, under the roof but open to the Watchman's Walk, was stored the big packing case that the cabinet organ had come in from Montgomery Ward. This packing case became my refuge when John took to playing with the school boys (I was not allowed to) and Mother was busy talking to her friends. Bored with their endless talk of babies and sickness and the goodness of God, I would climb up on this box and read Grimm's *Fairy Tales*, *The Swiss Family Robinson*, tales of the Greek gods and of the queens of England.

Three coffins were slung up high to the rafters in the front part of the walk. "It is mission property, church property. Church members have as much right to store things here as we," was Father's attitude about the coffins. The church members were treating the Ancestral Hall as their Ancestral Hall, as the headquarters of their club, as members of the guilds treated the temples where they had their headquarters. That was natural.

That there were three coffins showed there were three at least in the church whose families had enough money to provide for them before death.

The best coffin was Dr. Fan's. He owned a drugstore and practiced herb medicine in the Eastern Suburb, inside the wall of protection built when the "Long Haired Ones," the T'aip'ings who rebelled against the Manchu Dynasty from 1850 to 1865, were thought to be coming to our end of the province. He was the church member with the most money so naturally he was a deacon, but he was also a good man. Perhaps the Chang family of the Rear Village of the White Dragon was richer, but its wealth was in land. Anyway they could keep their coffins in their own farm compound. Furthermore old Mr. Chang was not a church member.

The second coffin was for Dr. Fan's wife.

The third coffin had been bought by Mr. Chu for his old father. Mr. Chu was the other deacon. He was Father's teacher. He had worked hard for that coffin, the sign of his filial piety and financial standing. To get together the money for that coffin had not been easy, what with his family growing so fast, the necessity to get a wife for his brother, and to gather the capital for his dairy.

Back near the coal house Father and Mother had had a swing hung from the rafters for John and me and for our friends. One day, I remember, Dr. Fan's two youngest daughters came to swing, while their father consulted with my father about church affairs. One was Lao Wu (The Fifth), the youngest of his own daughters. The other was Lu-te (Ruth), the daughter of his second wife, the widow, whom she had brought with her when she married Dr. Fan. They were much older than I. They were in their teens: thinking about the marriages being arranged for them. I stood and watched them, the little girl admiring the big ones.

Lao Wu was beautiful and vivacious as were all five daughters born to Dr. Fan by his first wife. She had classic features: the gently slanting eyes so few have and all admire, and the melon-seed shaped face with the provocatively pointed chin. Her chief beauty, however, was part of her chief problem. She had red hair, as did all five sisters, brick red hair. Red hair was not admired (demons of the underworld had such hair), but the fair skin and peach bloom cheeks that went with it were. Red hair could be dyed, but no one could bleach her skin to that tantalizing hue. Her feet were bound very small and daintily. Her oldest sister, Mrs. Tsang, and her second sister, Mrs. Chang, had both let their feet out, had taken off the bandages, early enough for them to be almost natural again. But Lao Wu was taking no chances. She was not giving up any bargaining point in the contract marriage that would be hers. The stepmother had come into the family at the right time to teach her the world- liness Dr. Fan was fast losing. Perhaps also Lao Wu thought bound feet beautiful.

The last time I saw Lao Wu, a few years later, she was sitting on the red marriage *k'ang* (the groom's family had borrowed part of the school dormitory, during the summer holidays, for the wedding), in the red marriage robes, her little red-shod feet tucked under her. The very next day her young husband took her away in a *shentse*, a mule litter, starting the five-day journey overland to Tsingtao. The English he had learned, that Mother had taught him, had secured for him an interpreter's job in that new port the Germans were building. I thought it inhuman to start off the very next day after a sleepless night. The hecklers, we heard, had stayed with them all night, both inside the house and outside their windows. The little demons that make trouble between husband and wife should forever have been driven away from this couple by their thoughtful friends, and much face gained by all.

The young groom did not do well, however, so Lao Wu spent most of her life in the old home village where her husband managed the estate his money-making brother built up. Perhaps bound feet were useful to her after all.

The village people were very conservative.

Lu-te, the other girl who came to swing that day, had come to Dr. Fan's family with her mother. Dr. Fan's first wife had borne him five daughters but no son. When she died (for being a church member he could not take a concubine to bear his wife a son, although the church-revered Abraham had done so), he took a new wife. She was a widow who had a son and a daughter. He wanted a wife who had proved she could produce a son. Widows, in old China, were not supposed to remarry. The saying used to teach their daughters was, "A horse does not carry two saddles: a woman does not marry two men." But widows did remarry. Economic necessity, too many women already in the family with another bread winner gone, or a lone woman, with no way to earn her living, made remarriage practical. If the widow had a son, the family into which he had been born would keep him. He was a future provider and one who could continue the family. The daughter, if there were one, would be sent away with the mother. She was but an added expense to any family bringing her up and a financial loss, as she would be married off into another family just as she was about to be useful. Accepting this added expense was part of the bride price for the new husband. Lu-te's mother had given Dr. Fan a son the first year, and he was content. He treated Lu-te in every way as his own daughter. She was known as Lao Liu, "The Sixth."

She also was beautiful. Hers was the "red and black" beauty, another much admired and more common type. Her rich black hair hung down her back in a heavy braid. The cheeks of her strong brown face were a deep bright red. But her destiny proved to be a bitter one.

One of the very best students in Mother's school was Gilbert Kao. Mother had given each boy an English name as soon as he started to study English. This was entirely in the scholarly tradition about which at that time I knew nothing. Each time a man entered a new field his friends gave him a new name. Gilbert Kao's family was a middling well-to-do farming family. He was going to continue his studies at the new college in Weihsien. He would be a teacher (that status the highest of all except to be an official) his family and hers felt sure.

He and Lu-te were married when I was away at school. I never saw her again, for he became assistant pastor of a church in the western part of the province. Later I was told about the young people's troubles. He became ill in his mind: "He became a child again, a baby. He would wear no clothes and his habits were those of a child who has not yet learned to care for himself," and Lu-te had to care for him. He was also a strong and vengeful baby. Lu-te hanged herself from the rafters. How could she know the nightmare would end and he become a devoted and devout pastor again?

But the shadow of boredom and the shadow of tragedy did not reach us that summer day (the school boys were away at wheat harvest or the girls would not have come) as the two young girls, almost women, worked the swing up together.

> "Red is the peach blossom, ah
> White is the winter orchid
> Swing we go up, ah
> Swing we go down
> And now together we turn."

They chanted as they swung up and down and made the difficult maneuver of changing sides when the swing, still moving, was at the lowest point.

Their finger nails were red, the bright Chinese red.

"How do you make your finger nails red?"

"Pulp the red blossoms of the lady slipper. Add a little alum. Tie a bit on each finger nail at night with a rag. They are red in the morning."

But Mother would not let me try. She said I must set a good example, that I must not be frivolous.

Every night we would hear the watchman in the compound next door (the one just like ours and separated from us by a wall only) as he made his rounds in the neighbor's Watchman's Walks and beat out the hours, the watches, that were as long as two of our hours. The hollow "bong bong" would sound dimly from their Eastern Walk, across their Entrance Court, get louder as he came down their Western Walk, and fade away again as he crossed the north end. Every two hours he made the rounds and beat out the time on his hollow sounding-wood, "bong bong."

We had no watchman making the rounds of our Watchman's Walks. We did not need one, Father said. We could not justify the expense. There was someone living in every court in our compound except in the Court of the Ancestors, and there was nothing to steal. As for telling the time, we had our clock and anyway we could listen to the number of beats made by the watchman next door.

The little gate in the north wall of the Watchman's Walks led to the Farm Courtyard. This was a great square courtyard with houses on three sides, the east, the west and the north. There was no house on the south, for it would have faced north and had no sunshine. That would not have been good for the overseer and the farm laborers who lived in this court, or for the grain that was stored, or for the horses, mules, and donkeys. With us there was no grain to store, and to stable there were only the donkey who turned the mill for the school boys and for a time the cow who gave milk for us children.

In the early days before Mother started the school, Dada and her family lived in the rooms in the southwest corner where the farm laborers had lived. The overseer's quarters in the southeast corner were used by visiting church members.

There was a well in the courtyard and a mill in the *chien* next to Dada's three rooms. In this Farm Courtyard the itinerant barber, who cared for the queues of the men in our compound—Father, Mr. Chu, Mr. Tsang, the head teacher and the other teachers, and the men servants, set up shop at regular intervals. It was like a party when the men gathered and sat, one by one, on the barber's red lacquer stool, while the others stood around in the bright sunshine and gossiped as they waited their turns. Fascinated, I would watch the barber take the copper basins, the iron razors, and the other implements of his trade from the round boxes he carried on either end of his pole. He gave massage, took wax out of ears and hairs out of nostrils, as well as shaved the heads and faces of the men and combed and braided their queues.

The barber would shave Father's hair the required inch back of the hair line, all around his head, and braid the rest of his hair which had been allowed to grow long. Father's queue was neither wispy like the cook's nor heavy and long like the washman's. To get some semblance of the correct width and weight into the braid, to accord with his dignity as a teacher, Father allowed the barber to braid into his hair a switch of long black silk cord. Most of the Chinese men braided switches of human hair into their queues, but Father would have none of that. A switch of cords could be seen for what it was and involved no pretense. Furthermore, though black to Americans, when seen beside Chinese hair, his was brown. Of course he would not let the barber dye his hair, much as the barber wished to. Father could not look like a Chinese but he could adopt their costume and their manners to remove as many obstacles to friendship with them as possible, to look and act as little queer to them as he could. China at that time was not a nation. It was a rich and well developed way of life. Those from outside who adopted that way of life were accepted, after a while, as inferior Chinese. Father even walked like a Chinese. How much that was conscious imitation, how much unconscious imitation, or how much because he wore Chinese shoes, I do not know. Perhaps all those factors entered in.

The Farm Courtyard seemed to Mother a perfect place for a boys' boarding school. In 1893, when I was five years old, she started one. There was none at that time in the whole mission. The one in P'eng-lai, where Mr. Chu (penniless and starving because his cart-driver father had smoked all his money away in opium) had been educated, was closed soon after I was born because of a schism in the mission. Some of the missionaries said it was not the responsibility of the missionaries to educate the Chinese or to provide them with medical care. These things, they said, the Chinese should do for themselves. The missionary's responsibility, they said, was to preach the Gospel of Jesus Christ and that only. Other missionaries said it was part of the responsibility inherent in the brotherhood of all mankind and expedient also that missionaries should run schools and clinics and hospitals. What better way to preach the Gospel than day-by-day to children at school or to the sick? This second group eventually won out. When the dissenters withdrew and formed the Gospel Mission in another province, Mother was free to open her school. And Mother loved to teach.

Mother was happy that she was able to increase the earning power of these boys who came to her school. She had no idea that in time some of them or their sons would call her an agent of imperialism. She was happy when her students got jobs as interpreters or accountants in Chefoo, the old treaty port, or in Tsingtao, the new port being developed by the Germans. Had she not taught them English and arithmetic, not part of the curriculum before? Was she not opening new doors to them and making it possible for them to add substantially to the family income and, she hoped, to see a wider world?

There was no student movement protesting the encroachments of the Western Powers in those days in our rural area. That was to come. Those who were antiforeign at that time hated the "Ocean People," the Western barbarians, for teaching ideas that, they said, undermined the family, teaching the young not to be filial and the women to demand equality.

The House of Those Who Must Also be Cared For was made into a dormitory. The stables and granaries were cleaned out, partitioned, and walls built in front, and made into more dormitories. The North Houses of the

Farm Court, those facing south, were made into class-
rooms, one on either side of the Back Gate. All day long
except for the periods when Mother taught English or
arithmetic, the boys shouted or droned their lessons as
they memorized the classics, each the part he was learning.
Repetition and more repetition until the passage was
forever fixed in his mind. When he thought he had a
passage secure he would go up to the teacher, hand him
his book, turn his back, and begin to recite. So the ordinary way to say he was reciting his lesson was to say he
was *pei shu*, "his back to his book." That there was a
school in a village could be known as far as the voices
could be heard, and the sound would be that of a giant
beehive. The overseer's quarters became the teacher's
house where Mr. Tsang, the Head Teacher, lived.

He was a very young Head Teacher and came from
the mountain village of Shang-chuang. He had the free
temper of the men of the hills and an adam's apple that
jerked as he spoke. In my imagination I could see him
striding up and down the hills. I thought the Prophet
Elijah must have looked something like him.

"Mr. Tsang has been fighting. His head is all bloody."

We raced to the schoolyard and saw Mr. Tsang just
coming in through the Back Gate. There were long bloody
scratches on his face and half of his hair seemed to have
been torn from his head. In his own hands he held a
handful of the other man's hair. In a fight, in those days,
the first maneuvering was toward seizing the opponent's
queue. Usually both succeeded. The fingernails, that all
wore as long as they could and still do their work, were
also very potent weapons.

It took all the diplomacy of that able negotiator, Mr. Chu, who was a schoolmate of Mr. Tsang's (and that meant almost a brother) as well as fellow church member, member of the same club, to settle the affair, to "talk harmony" and bring it to a proper conclusion. There was a big dinner, and everyone was satisfied.

I gathered, however, that it was very wrong to fight. One lost much face by fighting. One owned to a poverty of other means for settling whatever was disputed, especially one owned, by fighting, to a poverty of words with which to explain the principles of the matter and therefore to a poverty of the principles themselves. He who struck the first blow had already lost. He had owned to having no more arguments and so had proved that he was not in the pattern of harmonious living, in the rhythm of human relationships, did not know the logic of the pattern and was in the wrong.

That Mr. Tsang was one of the ablest men in the church was proved by the fact that he, a poor hill boy, married one of Dr. Fan's daughters. His temper also was turned into zeal. He later became the first Chinese pastor of the Huanghsien church.

In the Farm Court only the mill where the Ting family flour had been ground each day was left as it had been. A little furry donkey spent most of his life blindfolded and going around and around that mill, grinding the millet, corn, and soya beans for the boys' bread and wheat for their noodles.

John and I were jealous of the school. We said that Mother liked the boys better than she did us, that she spent more time with them than she did with us. The second was probably true. Instead of grumbling we would have done well to have gone to the school ourselves and to have learned to read and write the language of the people we were among. But we did not think of it and no one suggested it to us. No one among the missionaries then thought that a knowledge of written Chinese would be useful to any but missionaries and a few scholars, and who could be sure that their children would become missionaries or scholars when they were grown? If they did become missionaries later, they could learn to read enough to preach the Gospel as had their parents. I have always been sorry I was not taught to read and write Chinese in those years.

The Back Gate of the compound, the north gate, the Great Farm Gate, did not open as did the Great Front Gate—two huge doors that swung back on their pivots in wooden sockets and shut together again against the high heavy threshold. The Back Gate was a series of green-painted planks fitted into each other, as leaves of a dining table fit into each other, and placed on a less high threshold. The gate could be opened in sections according to the size of entrance needed for the loaded mules and donkeys. The whole could be cleared away for the heavy farm carts piled high with grain or even more bulky sorghum and corn stalks. A little door had been fitted into the last plank so people could come and go without opening the whole gate.

Outside the gate was an open space with a wall of tamped mud which had been the Ting family threshing floor. In the sunshine the scraps of wheat straw used for binding glistened like specks of gold and made us sorry for the Children of Israel who had to make bricks without straw.

During the two-month New Year season, when farmers had time for other things beside farming, travelling
entertainers made the rounds. Sometimes there would
come a man with a tiny trained monkey, shivering in his
little padded red coat, a trained dog and a sheep, who
would give a show in this space or inside the farmyard.
The monkey would end his performance by putting on a
series of masks—held in place by biting a little cross bar
inside—and posing as characters from the popular traditional operas and folk-tales, and then making a dashing
ride around the ring on the back of the sheep. I always
thought he looked very unhappy and frightened. Last of
all he passed the bowl into which we put the coppers. The
little dog, of course, knew more tricks and we liked him,
but the monkey was something we had never seen before
and looked so like a little old man. The little dog turned
a mill, among other things.

One year a team of sword players gave a show. I
did not like them. They seemed always about to kill
each other. I shut my eyes for the final act, and then
opened them again, my curiosity overcoming my fear.
They placed a square table—such as families ate around—
before us and on it they held a sword, blade up. The
men were very careful to call our attention to the sharpness
of the blade. They held two swords upright with the blades
facing inward. They completed the square with a sword
above, blade downward. The chief performer had to dive
through this aperture while the men holding the blades
made inward and downward thrusts as though to cut him
in half as he passed through, but his back was not even
scratched.

Outside the gate was the threshing floor. Between the threshing floor and the wall of the compound was our road to the highway that ran from our city to the sea and the rich villages of the plain. The highway was only four or five feet below the level of the threshing floor, for the Huanghsien roads were not deeply sunken. The land of the little coastal plain was almost level and the soil was not loess, that ancient wind-blown dust piled high over the northwestern provinces, where the roads were often deep ravines with vertical walls. Still our roads were always many feet enough below the fields on either side to give truth to the jingle: *"To nien ti tao lu tso ch'eng ho; To nien ti hsi fu ao ch'eng p'o* (The road of many years is walked into a river; the wife of many years is worked down into a mother-in-law)." Also the farmers dug up the road each year to catch all the fertilizing material left by the passing mules and donkeys, that had worked into the earth. When the road got too low and the banks on either side too high, the farmers were required to put some earth back into roads.

To have seen the farm carts laden with the harvest coming up the ramp from the highway to the threshing floor must have been a great thing. In the lesser glory of bringing the coal, brought by junks from the mines in the northeastern provinces and delivered at the little fishing village eighteen li away, and of bringing the boxes that came to us once a year from Montgomery Ward, we could see what the greater glory must have been.

"The carts are coming." I do not know who would make this announcement. Like the wind it passed through the compound. We all dropped whatever we were doing and rushed to the Back Gate and out to the ramp leading to the highway. The curtain wall around the threshing floor hid the carts as they came from the north, but we would get there in time to see them coming up the ramp. The muleteer sprang forward. He cracked his whip. He brandished it. He cracked it again. The lead mules swerved and turned up the ramp, making the wide sweep to give the mule in the shafts room to turn the cart.

The mules seemed to know they were at the end of their journey and to be proud of the job well done, or glad it was over. They threw up their heads. Their long manes and tails flew in the wind. They mounted the ramp in a gallant rush. For one brief moment they were not worn-out hacks. They were the noble beasts nature meant them to be.

8

DADA AND HER FAMILY

DADA WAS A MOST important person in our lives, almost as important as our parents. In some ways, perhaps, more important. She was with us all day, in all parts of the compound. I recognize many of my thoughts and attitudes as hers. She and her family must have a chapter to themselves. Dada was our amah, our nurse.

During the first years of my life Dada lived in the Farm Courtyard, in the three *chien* where the farm laborers had lived when the Ting family owned the compound. These three *chien* were like the conventional house of any ordinary family in our part of the country, but it opened into the Farm Court instead of into its own small courtyard. The only door was in the middle *chien*, the hallway, all-purpose room, and kitchen. The rooms on either side had each a wide *k'ang* under the window on which the family slept by night and sat by day. In the hallway-kitchen, against each bedroom wall, was a stationary cookstove, built of burnt brick and mud brick. A large round iron cooking basin was set in each of these stoves. The heat from the stoves while cooking went on to the flues under the *k'angs*, the brick beds, in the rooms beyond to warm them, and finally went with the smoke, up the chimneys. One of the favorite riddles of the people was about this domestic complex.

T'an t'an t'o	My head is round
Ssu fang yao	My body square
Yi chüeh yi pa	I lift my tail
Yi chang kao	A rod in the air

What am I?

Dada got us up in the mornings and saw that we washed our faces. We had no hair to comb or even brush, most of those years, as Mother kept our hair—John's, Ashley's, and mine—cropped short, even over our foreheads. "Saved trouble," she said. We called our nurse Dada because when she first came to us I could not say Ta Sao (Elder Sister-in-law), the honorary title by which we should have called her, and "Dada" could have been interpreted as calling her "Big-big." Everyone in the village called each other by some honorary title except the members of the Ting family and ours. The Ting family members were addressed as landlords and officials should be addressed, as Lao Yeh (Exalted Grandfather) and T'ait'ai (Great Exalted), while Father and Mother were addressed as a teacher and his wife, as Hsien-sheng (Born First) and Shih-niang (Teacher's Wife).

Dada always seemed old to me but she must have been in her late thirties and early forties those years she cared for us. The skin over her high cheek bones and full cheeks was smooth, though one side of her face caved in a bit where she had lost many teeth. Under the part of her forehead that had been added on her wedding day, her forehead was wrinkled while the added part was smooth and shone like a bald man's head. Every bride had this "addition" to her forehead made on her wedding day: had her hairline straightened by the bride's women. They twisted threads together and passed them over the bride's face and forehead. This pulled out all possible down on her face, preparing it for the application of the wet powder and the rouge. It also pulled out the hair immediately above her forehead to straighten the hairline so that it should be parallel with her brow and enlarge her forehead. On either side, vertically, in line with the outside ends of her eyebrows, the hair was pulled out to complete the square, high forehead. This high square space above the forehead was to a Chinese woman what the wedding ring was to her Western sisters.

Dada always wore the blue coat and trousers of the peasant: the coat was wide of sleeve and hung loosely to her knees, and the full trousers were caught into the garter at her ankle as were those of all women with bound feet.

Dada's feet were big. They were at least five inches long, for she came of a peasant family and had had to work around the compound and on the threshing floor even if she never went into the fields except to glean. Her feet had therefore not been bound as early as a city girl's or as tightly. I once saw one of her feet naked when she had to rewind the bandage. A woman did not lightly let anyone see her naked feet. The bandages that bound them were kept in a secret drawer of the low dressing table no

one else was allowed to open. Even her husband never saw
her bare feet. At night she took off her shoes and put on
her sleeping slippers, over the bandages. These were never
taken off except when she was alone. But Dada had a
sore spot on her foot that day. She sat on a box in the
Western Watchman's Walk and unwound the bandage
which was a good yard long or more. After all, I was a
very little girl.

The toes were turned under at the instep. Only the
big toe was in place, and the heel. The other toes were
atrophied and flattened up against the instep. The foot
was long and round, shaped like the horn of a young bull.
It was grey, inert, and stiff. Dada had no calf to her leg,
or not much. How could muscles develop that were
never used? So like hoofs were her feet. We could see
her calves were not developed when she rolled up her
trousers to her knees to make the flax into the twine she
used for sewing shoe soles. She would roll the flax on
her calf and then twist together several stands.

One day Dada took us to see a wedding at the house
next door, in the compound that was just like ours. The
compounds had been built by brothers, but the Ting
family of that compound still had money enough to
continue to live there. We crowded through the Great
Front Gate with half the village. We pushed through the
gate, across the Entrance Court, through the Second Gate,
and into the Court of the Ancestral Hall.

The courtyard was a solid mass of villagers on either
side of the Central Walk from the gate to the hall. The
music sounded. "They're bringing the chair through the
Great Gate," Dada said.

The music sounded again. Men hurried into the Court of the Ancestors with rolls of red felt in their arms. They laid a roll on the ground and pushed it ahead of them. It unrolled and made a red pathway.

The music changed. I could not see what was happening at the Second Gate: the crowd was too thick and I was too small. "The chair is at the Second Gate. They are taking the bride out," said Dada, pushing me forward between the people, to the edge of the red path down which the groom, dressed in his long blue silk robes, was coming. Over his silk robes was the purple bronze ceremonial coat. In each hand he held an end of one of the two long silk scarves of red silk. He was leading the bride, who held the other ends, as she followed him down the red path.

The men rolled out another felt in front of him. He passed on. Behind him, with a matron on either side holding her up, came the bride, walking down the red path.

The matrons had on black satin coats embroidered in all colors of the rainbow, and pleated red skirts from under which their tiny red shoes peeped. It was their duty to reassure the girl just leaving her own home, almost to carry her to the new home she must at least appear reluctant to enter.

The bride was a moving mass of red, from her tiny red shoes to the last ornament and pompom on her elaborate head dress. She was swathed in red: the color of happiness. Over her face was a square of red cloth. Above rose the towering intricate structure made up of the ornaments of gold and silver and kingfisher feathers that crowned her sleek black coiffure where her hair, for the first time in her life, was combed into a chignon. A wide red silk coat covered her entirely.

The groom mounted the steps to the Hall of the Ancestors. He entered the hall. The bride was helped up the steps. She entered the hall.

The villagers were turning and going out of the courtyard. They had seen the wedding procession. They had seen the spectacle of the red chair of the bride and the green chair of the bridegroom and the gay insignia carried through the streets. They were witnesses to the taking of the woman into the house of the Ting family. That was the marriage. The contract had been signed long ago when the engagement was made. This was the fulfillment of the contract. The bride had followed the groom into the Hall of the Ancestors and was now a member of his family. The villagers had seen the show and performed their function, that of witnesses. What went on inside the hall, when the groom and the bride kowtowed to his ancestors, both dead and living, was for the family and not the public.

"What do they do in the Hall of the Ancestors? Does someone marry them?" I asked, having seen my father perform marriage ceremonies for church members in our Ancestral Hall, now a church.

"No, they worship the ancestral tablets," and the subject was closed. I knew Dada would say no more. Ancestor worship was forbidden by the church, though Mother and Father said the people did not worship the ancestors in the same sense as Christians worshipped God, but that they venerated their ancestors. Dada did not always understand why she was required to do certain things, but she tried always to do what her employers wanted her to do when she was serving them. That was part of her integrity, both as a person and as a professional servant.

"Come, we'll go home now." Dada turned and started for the gate.

"I want to see more."

"No, there is no more for us to see."

I did not question why. We seldom questioned Dada's words. We had learned that she always had a reason for everything she did, one that we could accept. Usually she explained, but we had learned to watch her face: a purse of the lips, almost unnoticeable to anyone else, meant that she did not approve, meant "no"; a flick of the eye and we knew she meant for us not to do the thing we were doing, nor talk about it, at least not then.

"*T'a pu-li wo*" was the worst punishment for Chinese children. It was the worst punishment for us, all the punishment we needed from Dada. *T'a pu-li wo*—"She takes no notice of me," "Her face is turned aside from me." When the light of her countenance shone upon us the world was serene.

A lighter rebuke, when one had done something of which the elders disapproved, was *pu hai hsiu*, "not influenced by shame, not ashamed of doing what was not in the pattern, not afraid of the hurt of shame, did not fear to suffer shame." A purse of the maternal lips, a pointing finger, and the child had to be hard indeed not to feel the shame and stop what he was doing.

If Dada said "*Pu-shih jen*" of anyone, "Not a person, not acting like a human being," we knew she was harshly condemning. If we heard a mother on the street shout to her child, "*Pu-shih jen*," we knew she was really angry with him. *Pu-shih jen*, used by an adult to an adult, was highly insulting and could lead to a fight. *Pu-shih jen*, "not a human being, acting like a creature with four legs instead of a human being with two, one who could not think and take responsibility.

Ch'eng jen, "become a human being, a reasoning being," was to praise a child, to acknowledge that the process of development had become apparent. This was normally expected to show forth in the seventh year. Furthermore, it was the quality of being human that was important. Even women were human beings (*jen*) first, and female beings (*nü jen*) second. Men were *nan jen*, "male human beings." Good people were *hao jen*, "good human beings"; and bad people were *huai jen*, "bad human beings." So was built up in me, as in Chinese children, the conviction of the dignity and worth of the human being.

Dada's husband, Chiang Wen-chi, was our cook. Marketing and cooking was a fulltime job when everything to be eaten had to be bought fresh every day at a market in the western suburb, half an hour's walk away, and cooked over a cumbersome coal stove. The trip to the grain shop, which along with the pawn shops were the banks of the period, to get the money needed also took time, as they were inside the walled city. He reigned in the kitchen, the three-*chien* house (one *chien* partitioned off for the pantry) against the east wall of the Court of Those Who Also Must Be Cared For. It had been a kitchen and maids' room in the time of the Tings.

"Shoo, get out. You're all nuisances," and he would flap the dish cloth at us.

We liked to beg tidbits from the kitchen, but we had learned we could get nothing without Dada along. The kitchen was best when Mother made doughnuts (deep fat took away the curse of fried things) or marble cake, as she did once in a long time and when she was sure that Chiang Wen-chi would be away for half a day. She would let us scrape the mixing bowl.

If Chiang Wen-chi was in a good humor Dada would take us to the kitchen and sit in an old chair against the east wall and talk with him while he prepared our food on the table in front of the west-facing window or fussed around the stove against the north wall.

"Huh! Imagine people like that calling themselves Chinese!" He was telling Dada for the hundredth time the story of the trip he had taken with my father and mother to Shanghai. He scorned the people there. "They could not even speak Chinese. I said to the Mistress, 'Let's go home. Let's go back where the people are Chinese.'"

He was always bristling and arguing. He sounded like a noisy rooster. His thin little queue, that reached only to his shoulder blades, jerked as he talked and his Adam's apple bobbed up and down in his long thin neck. His little thin face was permanently screwed up.

"Shoo, I'm going to kill the chicken and you know your mother does not like you to watch." Often he said "Shoo" without that amount of excuse, but I would run for I did not like to see the chickens flopping around the court with the blood gushing from the ragged gap in their throats.

"Rats eat that evil-smelling stuff!" said he, holding the cheese from the Montgomery Ward box at arm's length and turning his head away in disgust. "Perhaps American rats will eat it. No Chinese rat would." He lost much face

over the matter for he did not put the cheese, that had
come all the way from America, into a rat-proof container.
He found that rats the world over had the same tastes.

"Put salt into the ice! What a waste of good salt!"
Salt was a government monopoly. Salt cost a great deal
of money. Salt was a human necessity. Waste salt on an
ice cream freezer!

We had ice cream in winters only, until Mr. Stephens,
the new missionary who came when I was six, put up an
icehouse. Before that, trying to give us children an idea
of the delicacy so much enjoyed in America, we had snow
cream, newly fallen snow mixed with milk and sugar and
flavoring extract. Then, when the new freezer came from
Montgomery Ward, the cook, under protest, set out pans
of water and collected the ice for the great new dish those
crazy people from across the ocean seemed to want to
eat. "Imagine liking to eat anything cold—taking things
as cold as that into one's stomach. Sure to make one ill."

Neither Chiang Wen-chi nor his countrymen had ever
heard of germs, but they had learned from millenia of experience that those who were careful to eat only hot food
did not become ill as often as those who ate cold food. It
was therefore deduced that it was the quality of coldness
in the food that made one ill. No stranger than the idea
that night air in a swampy country caused malaria.

Grumbling, he put the ice in the new freezer around
the container with the custard mixture. What seemed
hours later, when we should have had the ice cream long
since, he was found in the windiest corner of the compound furiously turning the crank of the freezer with no
salt on the ice.

We did not have ice cream often. It would have seemed too wasteful to the villagers—wasteful and ostentatiously wasteful to have used up so much salt, even though Mother had the cook save the water and let it evaporate and so regain some of the salt.

The kitchen at times was a family conclave, for the "boy" was a member of the family also. He was their son. His main duties were to wait on table, do our laundry, and keep the various jars and pitchers in the house full of water. He also worked in the little garden Mother had made in one corner of the courtyard across from the kitchen.

I liked to watch the "boy" (we called him by his name Chiang Te-ts'ung) draw water from the well as he turned the windlass on its tripod of stripped poles, his muscles smooth bands under the golden brown skin of his arms and back and calves, set off by his indigo blue trousers rolled up to his knees. As he drew the water and turned it into the great Ali Baba jars or carried the buckets across the court, slung on either end of his pole, his movements were like a dance: the rhythm, footwork, and design in the bending and the lifting as he turned the windlass, lifted the bucket, and poured out the water. There was counterpoint and emphasis in the lordly stance as he lowered the bucket into the well, one arm outstretched with the hand on the windlass, breaking the speed, proud of his control and prowess.

When our washman set the table, for his duties were varied, and waited on us as we ate, his queue would be hanging down his back in respect for his employers and in respect for himself as one who knew the right thing to do and did it at the right time. When he washed the dishes in the kitchen or clothes in the laundry, his queue would be coiled around his head to get it out of the way. Mother tried not to go to the kitchen or washhouse when he was working, as he would then have to stop what he was doing and push the braid off his head so it would hang down his back.

He also rang the bell that called us to meals. It was an American bell from Montgomery Ward. I tried not to hate it, for it was an American bell, but I hated its raucous tones. I always hastened to obey its summons and urged John and Ashley, for it would not stop until we got there. I think the washman liked to ring it. It gave him command over us. Also it made a lot of noise.

Most of the day he was in the washhouse, the little three *chien* house against the west wall in the Women's Court. He lived in one of the *chien* until his family leased land and moved into their new house in the village. He heated water for the washing in the great set-in iron cooking basin in the central *chien*. The earthenware tubs were there also, set on heavy wooden stools. This house must have been one of the kitchens when the Ting family lived in our compound and where some of the maids slept. In the third *chien* he ironed on a long table.

The washman reigned in this house. He did not shoo us away as did his father. He ignored us. That was even more effective and we did not often go to see him. Sometimes we went with Dada. Standing by the ironing board with his back to us he would not acknowledge our presence until Dada spoke to him.

"Not fart? Why should I not fart?" The washman was being argumentative.

"They don't like it," said Dada.

"Why don't they like it?"

"It makes a smell."

"A fart with a noise does not make a smell," said he, demonstrating, "only a fart without a sound. It is strange that it should be so."

Dada gave up and took us away. Dada was very patient.

She took us back to the kitchen court. We passed through the living room and the dining room and out through the pantry. That was the shortest way from the Women's Court to the Court of Those Who Must Also be Cared For. The pantry was part of what had been storage space for the Tings, north space that balanced the veranda in front, on the south, and helped keep out the cold north winds in winter.

Only once do I remember feeling any emotion in Dada and it was in this pantry. It was summer and we all had what was known as "summer complaint." Even the wide pieces of flannel we all wore around our middles to guard against the chills that came with the sudden drops in temperature and caused diarrhea, according to the then current belief, had not been able to save us that summer. (That those pieces of flannel were called "cholera belts" by the Westerners showed that the germ theory had not taken too strong a hold on them.) Fresh fruit was therefore forbidden us. We were not allowed to eat it that whole season. We were hungry for fruit. Whether Dada, with her wisdom of the ages, knew that our systems needed fruit, or whether she thought Mother was keeping it from us for some secret satisfaction of her own, or whether she was getting back at Mother for something in her own relationship to Mother, I will never know. The bowl of fruit—peaches, apricots, and pears—for Father and Mother, had been put on the top shelf beyond our reach. Dada tensed suddenly, reached up and took a peach for each of us. She helped us peel them and kept a watch out while we ate. And her face was hard.

When my little brother Ashley died of diphtheria at the age of six and there was no baby left in our house, Mother let Dada go to Mrs. Stephens, to care for her baby. I was never happy about that. I did not like my Dada leaving us to care for anyone else. But even more than my feelings were the feelings of those around me. A nurse, a second mother to a child, stayed the rest of her life with the child even as the child's own mother stayed. Poverty only could excuse sending the nurse-mother away. I doubt that my parents knew of this part of the pattern. I certainly did not know it then, but I felt it. For many years I did not see much of Dada, especially as the family had moved, when the school was opened, to a house in the village.

They told us Dada had died. We went to see her. She lay stiff on the improvised bed of planks on benches, in the common room of their home in the village. We knew that all who were dying had to be removed from the *k'ang*, the brick bed, to die on a wooden bed (or plank or door taken from its pivots if the people were poor). Dada was a Christian, a church member, and therefore would not believe that she would have to carry a big mud brick on her back throughout the stages of judgment in the next world should she have died on the *k'ang*; but it was the custom to die on a wooden bed and her family had moved her. We could see her face, turned a little to the west as she lay with her head to the north. It was as though she were sleeping.

As we went out the door we saw Chiang Wen-chi who had, so many years before, been our cook. His little queue was even slighter than before and he was very thin. Dada had learned her vast patience as much from listening to his endless opinions about everything as she had from tending so many foreign children. But this day he had nothing to say. He shook his old head. "There is no flavor left now to life." We knew he meant since her death. The doctor said there was nothing the matter with him—that he had no disease a doctor could describe and treat—but in a few weeks he was dead.

When my little brother Robert was born, Mother had to get him a new Dada. I liked her. She was not as kind and thoughtful as my Dada had been but she was more talkative. She would tell us stories. And she did not seem to mind my young curiosity. She had a son named Tao-tzu, "Upside down." I wanted to know why he was called "Upside down."

"They hung the bow on the gate upside down when he was born."

"Why did they hang a bow?"

"To tell that a son was born in that home."

She mentioned her bitter destiny so often that I asked her about it. "Why is your destiny bitter?" She did not have a mother-in-law, had never had one; her husband's mother had been dead when she went to him a bride. But a mother-in-law was the most common bitter destiny I heard about among women in our rich part of the province. Mothers-in-law for women and debts for men.

"Ah, you don't know, Little Mistress. Look at me. Look at the clothes I wear." They were the usual blue

cotton coat and trousers of the Shantung woman, whether
living in the city, the market town, or the country, for
the ordinary housewife. They were faded and had been
worn a long time. "And look at the clothes my brother's
wife wears." Her brother had been educated in the mission
school and was a teacher of the classics, and his wife was
one of the educated women, rare at the time. She taught
English, very popular at the time, and earned much
money. If the new Dada was jealous, it was so old a
jealousy that it had sunk into the deep recesses of her
heart. It was her destiny to be poor, a destiny determined
no one knew how many lives before the present life. She
could but accept her destiny and make the best of it, so
that in the next incarnation she would have expiated more
of her previous mistakes and crimes (again, probably many
lives before) and so be able to live a more comfortable
life. Destiny was determined, but part of the determined
destiny was the ability to strive, which, if not used, left
the destiny incomplete. She was not bitter. She was but
showing the difference between her destiny and that of
her sister-in-law.

"All my life I have worked in the fields. Look at my
feet. Are those the feet of a woman of fortunate destiny?
Spread to this size? Should a woman work in the fields
pulling the plow beside the ox? Should there not be a
donkey?"

I knew that in our part of the country women were
not supposed to work in the fields and it did not often
happen. That was man's work. For a woman to work in
the fields the family had to be poor indeed. Her brother
was a teacher, an educated man. That she had been
married to a farmer was not strange. That happened to

most women in Shantung Province, in all China, where farmers were over eighty or ninety percent of the population, but to be married to a poor farmer. . . .

"How did it come about that you were so poor? Your brother is a scholar."

"*Ai*! we were cheated by the matchmaker. Both my sister and I were cheated by the matchmaker. The matchmaker told my father and mother that the Liu family had much land. He did not tell us that most of it was rocky hillside, and even at that it was not as much as the matchmaker said. Even if had it been only half as much as the matchmaker said, had it been level farmland, we could have been well off enough." She smiled. The bitterness was passed. "I cried all the first year I was married. I had never done such hard work. But then I saw that my destiny was bitter so why cry. Also I had my son to watch over."

"You have been fortunate in that respect, at least," I said to be comforting. "You have two sons and that is a good destiny."

"*Hai*! You don't know. I had six girls."

"Where are they?" I said, opening my eyes in surprise.

"Dead. I killed them all. I choked them to death with my own hands. When each child was born I said to the midwife, 'What is it?' and if she said 'A boy,' I took it into my arms and nursed it. If she said it was a girl, I held out my hands but I would not look at it. If I had looked at it I would have loved it and could not have done what I had to do. I choked the life out of it. How could we feed so many mouths?"

Even then I knew that a boy was an investment that would repay his parents in work after a very few years, in care of them in their old age and in the life to come, while a girl was an investment that benefitted only the other family, the one she went to as soon as she was beginning to be able to work.

1. Author's father, C.W. Pruitt, in his twenties (sometime in the 1880's).

2. Father's teacher.

3. Father's teacher's wife, who bore fifteen children and
raised five.

4. Chao Teh-shan, the herd boy who became an official.

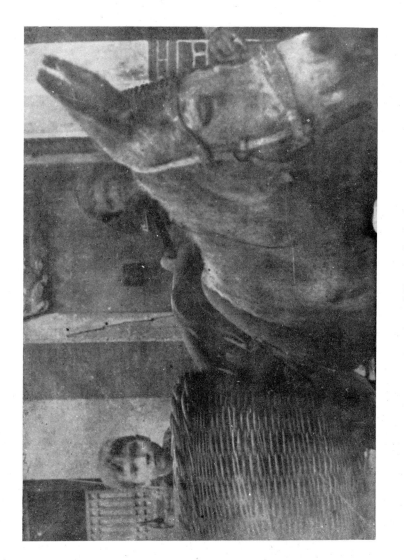

5. Author and brother riding in baskets on a donkey.

6. Mule-litter—usual mode of travel for any distance.

7. The family starting to P'eng-lai. Mother and author in a sedan-chair, father on a donkey. Dada also on a donkey behind father, upper right, with Mr. Chu below her. Second figure from the left is Chiang Wen-chi, the cook.

9

OUTSIDE THE GREAT FRONT GATE

TO BE OLDER AND have longer legs was good. We could go outside the Great Front Gate. That was fun. Our world was enlarged.

We could go to the cool cave of the Great Front Gate which was as deep as the Street House was wide. Since the gatekeeper lived in the *chien* next to the gate cave and since he was always there, the gate was always open, all day long. We would not need to get someone to lift the heavy beam from across the two leaves of the gate, lift it out of its wooden sockets, nor slide back the heavy bolts of wood. For years, however, it took an effort to step over the high threshold.

The threshold was a good place to sit and wait for the *tou-fu nao* man, the man who sold the steaming soybean curd, fresh from its overnight slow cooking, and the thick savory soup that was poured over it. Away back in the compound we could hear the sound of his gong—a plate of brass about six inches long and four inches wide on which he beat with a padded ball on the end of a stick. We knew that sound. John and I would rush for our bowls and chopsticks and the three coppers it took to buy the bowlful of *tou-fu nao* and soup. The coppers were dirty, we knew, but copper was said to kill the germs so we carried them, as did everyone else, in the bottom of our bowls. And then we would run as fast as we could to the Great Front Gate.

Down the street he came from the eastern end of the village toward us at the western end, stopping at intervals as customers hailed him. As we sat on the high wooden threshold, waiting, we could hear the sounds of the village to which, in our busy life of play, we had not listened or could not hear back in the compound: the birds in the trees of the Ting family garden across the street and the cicadas; the dogs barking as someone went to a gate; the rhythmic, muffled, staccato click as the women beat their clothes smooth—dampened and folded and laid on the little polished stone stools made for the purpose, beat them with two highly polished hardwood beaters; the sharp thud of the stone mason's chisel as he sharpened someone's millstone; perhaps a donkey braying. All else was silence or the hum that is silence, the hum that is made up of all these things, and of human voices too far away to be distinguished, and the grinding of the cart wheels in the ruts of the roads, and the pat of the many cloth-soled shoes on the beaten earthen paths.

One day as we sat waiting for the *tou-fu nao* man we saw Dada's sixteen-year-old daughter, Wen-tzu, coming down the street. She was Dada's youngest child. Dada and her husband had had as many children as they wanted by the time she was born—two boys, and this one was the second girl. So they named her Wen-tzu, "to stop," "to lay away," and they had no more children. I knew another little girl whose name was Kai-erh, "to change." They wanted the next child to be of the other sex, and he was.

Dada had not bound Wen-tzu's feet, for it was against the ideas of the church to bind girl's feet. It was too early for it to be a rule. There was no use to make rules that could not be kept except in what was considered absolute essentials such as ancestor worship. The Bible said nothing about bound feet, but it did say there should be "no other God before Me." Wen-tzu was not happy about her big feet and was resentful toward her parents for not having bound her feet when she was six or seven. The natural feet made her conspicuous, she said. "They call me prostitute (this was because many of the girls, slave girls used for the trade, did not have their feet bound) and they revile me," she would weep. "With such big feet how will I ever get a mother-in-law?" To find a mother-in-law's family was the ordinary expression for getting married. Wen-tzu tried to walk as those who had bound feet walked, to walk as a woman should walk. But she wore the wide trousers, not tied in at the ankle, of the women whose feet were not bound, and she could not, try as she would, mince and make her body sway as the bound footed women minced and swayed.

Suddenly, as I sat there and watched her walking toward me I saw the bound foot as very beautiful, tiny and dainty, and shaped like the horn of a young bull. Clothed in the delicate embroidered shoes, they made perfect and harmonious stems for the swaying beauty of the whole woman. As I watched Wen-tzu, in her everyday cotton clothes, walking down the street, I could see that other woman. I could see her from the tiny shoes to the shining black hair lying close to the head and dressed into the tightly coiled chignon or butterfly or braid. Matrons would have bound across the forehead the black satin band for a hat on which were sewn jade and silver ornaments. They would be dressed in the wide-sleeved coat of bright color with the deep, black satin yoke and the deep, black satin cuffs, banded with brocade ribbon; the trousers of another but equally pleasing and complementary hue. I was seeing with Wen-tzu's eyes. I was sorry for Wen-tzu as she was for herself.

That was the only time bound feet looked beautiful to me. I was thinking Chinese thoughts, centuries old. Of course I knew nothing about the aphrodisiac quality of the tiny feet for the men of the time. I doubt Wen-tzu did either. She was concerned with what concerned all girls in the agriculture-handicraft era, in whatever country they lived: with getting married, securing a family, a settlement in life. The life of a servant, a prostitute, a nun were the only alternatives.

As the *tou-fu nao* man came down the street and neared our gate we would shout. He would slide the carrying pole off his shoulders and place his loads on the street, on the round old millstones that had been placed there for the carts to run on and for the bearers who carried the wedding chairs to strut on. These millstones paved the village street at our end of the village. On either side, also at our end of the village, were wide sidewalks paved with field stone. Few carts came through our village and fewer wedding processions. If a cart came along or a sedan chair it could wait while the *tou-fu nao* man moved his loads to the sidewalk—but none came.

The load at one end of his pole was a series of trays about two feet in diameter and six inches deep, fitted together into a round box between three and four feet high. On these trays were kept his bowls and chopsticks, the condiments he used, and the charcoal for the fire. On top was a little stove with a wide, shallow iron basin in which the soup was kept always hot. On the other end of the pole was a deep earthen pot in which the *tou-fu*, the soybean curd, had been cooked all night over a slow fire.

The *tou-fu nao* man had a beaming smile on his thin expressive face. With a flourish he lifted the wooden lid off the big pot, and we watched the warm steam rise in a mist to his face. With a sweep of the other arm he sliced the flat copper ladle into the *tou-fu nao* and dished up a quivering white clabberlike mass with the faint sweet smell of the bean. In one or two exaggerated steps—mincing and swaying and strutting—such as stage figures, playing clowns or servants, use to show a mixture of deference and independence, he walked to the other end of the pole. With a big shallow copper spoon he ladled the thick clear soup in which floated all manner of interesting tidbits, tiny green leaves of a savory vegetable, the *yeh-hsi ts'ai*, specks of egg, tiny slices of ham, the deer antler seaweed, and poured it over the *tou-fu*, the beancurd. On top of all he would throw a few tiny dry salt shrimps. The pungeant savory fragrance steamed gently upward as we carried the bowls carefully with both hands, back to the gate, to sit on the threshold and eat.

Throwing the coppers we had handed him into a tray by the cauldron, the *tou-fu nao* man would lift the pole to his shoulder and swagger down the street to the highway.

Sometimes in the afternoon (the *tou-fu nao* man came in the morning) we would hear the bean-pastry man call. His call started low as he said *Tou-erh*, "bean" and went lower still on his first *"pei"* and rose to the second. *Pei-pei* was a steamed pastry most often solid but sometimes with various fillings. It could be meat and vegetables chopped together, or it could be sugar, flavored with ginger and rose leaves and glazed plums, or it could be bean paste.

But the *pei-pei* man was deaf and did not always hear us call him when, having run half the length of the compound, we reached the street to see him about to turn the corner into the highway, his basket of pastries, covered with a damp cloth that had once been white and was now grey, on his shoulder. He would be surly if we caught him and grudgingly sell us as many of the pastries as we paid for. Perhaps he was surly because he was deaf. Perhaps he did not like the "ocean people," the foreigners, whom he probably called "foreign devils." Dada never encouraged us to buy from him. Perhaps that also might have been because Mother thought the rich bean paste not good for us.

From the Great Front Gate to the highway, which was at right angle to our village street, was the front wall of our compound. This was also the back of the House of the Entrance Court. This street wall was of grey burnt brick up to the eaves, blank of any window. At regular intervals, at the height of a man's chest, were six or eight heavy iron rings, about six inches in diameter, attached to iron staples driven into wooden blocks set in the wall. To these had been hitched, in the old days, the mules and horses ridden by the men who visited Mr. Ting, and the mules that had drawn the carts of the women who had visited the Ting women. I never saw the rings in use outside our compound, although I saw mules and horses tied to those across the street and next door. The church members who did not come on foot would leave their mules and donkeys in the school courtyard, the Farm Courtyard. They had no grooms to tend the animals while they were at the services.

The highway was a fairly important one, but since it was not a trunk road from one *hsien* city to another it was not an official highway. It went from the North Gate of the walled city of Huanghsien to the rich farms in the flat lands between the city and the sea, some of the richest land in our rich *hsien* or district.

A row of poplar trees, tall and majestic, grew on the east side of this highway toward the city. In the distance, like a background not clearly seen, was that long low line of the Wall of Protection, crenelated against the sky, and the low tower over the North Gate. This second wall had been built by the rich merchants of the four suburbs, to surround their homes and businesses that clustered outside the four gates of the city, when they thought the Long Haired Ones were coming. The Wall of Protection looked like a city wall. It was as high and wide but had been built of tamped earth plastered over with lime and sand that had turned black with the years. The city wall, like an inner shell to the city, was built of stone bricks. Many of the old villages in the plain had smaller Walls of Protection built at that time, which had become crumbling mounds of earth.

"Mother," I asked, when I learned that American cities did not have walls, "how do you know when you are in the city?"

Farm carts, heavily laden with grain, ground by to the market in the city, or to the big market in the west suburb, the wheels jolting in the ruts and piling up little mountain ranges of soft black earth on either side. I liked to take off my shoes and stockings to paddle in the soft thick dust until Mother caught me and forbade the practice. She spoke darkly of hookworms and other unpleasant things the doctor had told her about.

Family carts with sedan frames pulled at a quick trot by fat mules, usually black, would pass by. If the curtain was down, there was a young woman inside, member of a rich family in one of the villages to the north. If it was a man or an old woman inside, the curtain would be up so they could see what there was to see and not have to depend on the tiny window of silk gauze or glass set into the curtain. Sitting crosslegged with grave dignity, they seemed to pay no attention to the queerly dressed brats with their white faces and pale hair, though probably they missed no detail.

Best of all to me were the young bloods going to the city for a day or night of pleasure, or returning to their homes in the great compounds of the villages. To tell which was more beautiful was very difficult, the man or the mule. They really had to be taken as one—were meant to be so taken.

The mules were always black and fat, their rumps sleek and rounded. They did not seem to belong to the same species as the brown and grey and white mules with sunken rumps and hammer necks that carried the mule litters we rode in, or like the farm mules and donkeys which were adequately fed but on whom not much time was spent. The hides of these mules the young men rode were groomed until they shone. The harness and saddles were decorated with shining metal, the bells around their necks clashed and jingled, making sure that we should see them as they paced proudly by. For they all paced. That was the favored gait. Their manes and tails, into which were braided red cords, flew free in the wind.

The men, young men, dashing young men, sat their high saddles in a fashionable slouch. Even the barbarian little girl could see that. Their knees were high and bent. Their long silk gowns, split up the back to fall on either side of the saddle, were blue or black with gay short sleeveless overjackets of bronze or blue or red, while the ends of their bright sashes showed beneath. The crowning glory was their hair, great thick braids, the ends of which they tucked into their girdles to keep them from swinging as they rode.

"*Pan t'iao tzu*, half a string of cash," someone would mutter as they passed in groups of two or three. "Half a string of cash! Not much good! Not worth much! Young wasters, young landlords." Sometimes the braid in their queues did not begin until well down on their shoulders, between the shoulder blades. The braids of respectable young men started against their shaved heads. Starting on the neck was smart and a daring act allowed even to the respectable. But halfway down their backs? Dissolute indeed!

They were, however, very beautiful, I thought.

"*Pan t'iao tzu*, half a string of cash." The village blades had the same low-braided queues though not as well kept, nor could their cotton garments achieve the style of the young lordlings' silk. They made up for it by leaving their collars insolently open. Their swagger on foot was of the same quality as the style with which the young blades sat their mules. The impassive arrogance of the young lordlings could easily have broken into the robust songs—almost always ribald and more than often lewd—the village blades sang as they walked along the foot paths above the highway. The frowns of the respectable when they heard these songs, the only ones they knew, made a hurdle for the missionaries teaching the singing of hymns.

I never heard any of them, either the young bloods or the village yokels, called *hao han-tzu*, as I heard the village women call the young men at work or sturdy small boys. I can see the gleam in the eyes of the old women as they watched the brawny bare shoulders of the carpenters sawing the great logs or a farmer working in the fields or a carter managing his mules. I soon learned that to be a *hao han-tzu* one must have character as well as a good body and a handsome face. This was not formulated in my mind, it became a part of me. Also, I was grown before I realized that *hao han-tzu* could not be literally translated as "fine young man," but that the people were harking back to the great Han Dynasty (200 B.C.–A.D. 220) and calling their good and stalwart young men "Fine Sons of Han."

We saw farm women go riding by on donkeys or plow mules, usually with a child in front and sometimes one behind also, the mothers' faces, if they were young, white with powder applied wet and cheeks bright red with rouge, cerise flowers stuck in their black chignons. A husband or a brother plodded along in the dust, carrying a little whip, and perhaps a bundle of her clothes.

We saw many wedding processions going up or down that road, the groom in the green chair and the bride in the red, and the little procession of musicians and those carrying banners.

We saw many funerals on their way from the city to the graveyards scattered all over the land. In winter when there were no crops to hide the mounds, the land looked as though great armies of outsized gophers had taken over the country, or as if the hills had shrunk to little mounds and invaded the plain. Everywhere one could see the little mounds, sometimes not so little, until the eye got used to them and they were no longer there. Always the living and the dead were close to each other.

"The T'ai Lai funeral is passing." I do not know who said it. Some sharp ears must have heard the gongs and cymbals and horns as the procession began to come out of the city. All knew the funeral was to be this day. Whoever heard a piece of news passed it on. The duty of the next was to pass it further. I could never pass on such news as casually as it came to me. I would jump up and down with impatient energy, shouting to John and Dada and Ashley to hurry.

The first of the procession had already passed when we got to the highway, but that did not matter, for it was a mile long and would take almost an hour as the bearers straggled by. There was every kind of funeral decoration and insignia, all that retainers of the old lords had carried in the very old days, now carried by beggars with the rented funeral-house coats only half concealing their rags or worn clothes. The beggars—they were not too numerous

in rich Huan-hsien—and half beggars and the poor of the
city must have eaten well for many days after that funeral.

Red and gold and blue and green but mostly red and
gold, the procession passed by in the slightly sunken road
while we stood on the bank, on the footpath, and watched
and listened. We stood by the end of the long curtain
wall, the spirit screen for the village which protected the
open end of the village and stretched, on the other side
of the highway, across the end of the village street and
down the full length of our compound.

The T'ai Lai funeral was that of an old woman. T'ai
Lai, the name of the greatest pawn shop or series of pawn
shops in Huang-hsien, was owned by the wealthiest branch
of the Ting family which was the wealthiest family of the
district. Pawn shops were the banks of the period. The
Ting family, therefore, owned much land as well as
fabulous stores of silver. Stories of great rooms piled
high with silver ingots floated through the air. The legendary beginnings of the family had already become a
part of the folklore of the countryside. The story was
known to everyone who sat on a *k'ang* and gossiped. A
hundred years ago, perhaps, no one was very certain about
the lapse of time, famine refugees—an old man and his
daughter-in-law, far gone with child, all that were left of
a large family—had arrived in a Huang-hsien village. The
villagers had tried to make them comfortable, had given
them food and built them a hut to shelter them from the
winter storms, a place dry and warm. That the villagers,
for the hut, should have roofed over the hole left in the
ground when a great tree overturned and tore out its roots,
was not strange. There was a racial memory, a memory
handed down in tradition, in a culture unbroken for many

thousands of years, of the round dugout houses, roofed with thatch, of their ancient ancestors. Also did not people still live in caves in the loess land? Here in this thatch-covered pit the woman's child had been born and the old man died. There where he lay they had buried the old man, filled in the pit and raised the mound over him. The young one, who started life as a beggar, grew up to become fabulously wealthy. There was luck and magic and a willful girl in the story and a hidden cache of silver ingots found in the hills. Everyone knew enough of the laws of Wind and Water to know, of course, that the cause of his good fortune had been his grandfather's burial in one of the veins of the earth through which good currents flow, the vein which had been opened by the overturn of the great tree. So strong was this good current, this current of fortune, that the family had been wealthy for many generations.

This fortune was now running out, however, and because of another willful woman. Many tales were told of the old woman they were now burying, of the dissolute life she had led when she was a dowager but not an old woman. Most of the tales dealt with her lovers and how she had dissipated the estate to pay them, and of the great lawsuits waged against her by members of the Ting family to try to stop her but which had further reduced the family estate. "Why should she care? She was not a Ting. She had only wedded one. Why should she not enjoy what she could?"

Her son hated her. In the last years of her life, she would eat nothing not first tasted in her presence. She kept slave girls for that purpose, it was said.

Once also on this road we saw a *hsiu ts'ai*, a young scholar who had passed his first official examination, making his triumphal ride, the ride in which he announced to the world he had received the first degree, the ride in which he dressed as an official for the first time and perhaps for the last time in his life. Many of the young *hsiu ts'ai* never got any official post and spent their lives as village schoolmasters. We saw him in his embroidered robes, with the high hat and the red tassels, riding a horse. An attendant carrying an embroidered state umbrella walked beside him.

Usually what we saw were farmers swinging down the foot paths with their produce in baskets at either end of their poles. The loads were heavy but not too heavy for the farmers to take pride in their prowess. He who belonged to a family, had a bit of land and health, could live, and not too poorly, and not work too hard in our rich coastal plain. The land, for the most part, was in small holdings and where they were leased from landlords, the terms did not seem to be exorbitant. Most people seemed to have enough to eat, but we heard much about debts. There were also journeymen walking to their tasks. "I can tell the occupation of any man by the way he walks, even from behind," said Mr. Chu. A common sight was that of an old man and a little boy, each with an iron ladle and a basket, picking up animal droppings along the highway to add to the family compost pile: the grandson beginning to take up the work on the land and the grandfather tapering away from work.

When Ashley was old enough to walk Dada would take us out the Great Front Gate and across the highway, up the little bank to the footpath across the fields to the

Ting family cemetery, the cemetery of our branch of the Ting family. It was square and had a wall on three sides, the open side to the south. The wall was finished with a deep border of tile lace work. Behind the wall, on the three sides, were poplars and pines, tall and straight. The mounds were large, much larger than the mounds of the people who buried their dead in their grain fields, but not as large as they should have been, for earth had not been added each year in the spring and autumn solstices, as was proper. The mounds rose as the swelling breasts of the Great Earth Mother over the womb, over the wombs, that held her children forever.

Perhaps the Ting family came, as other families did to the graves all around, to serve and worship their ancestors, to bring food and clothing to those who were now on the other side of the invisible curtain, but who needed food and clothes and affection. But we never saw on those graves the little carrot lamps, sections of carrots scooped out and filled with oil, which rode like little armies up the other graves after the fifteenth of the seventh moon. That was the day of All Souls, on which the spirits visited their old homes, supposedly for the day, and were lighted back to their earth homes in the evening by their descendants. Often this journey back to the graves was taken in the early afternoon, the convoying relatives carrying lighted lanterns, the spirits supposed not to be able to tell the difference between day and night, and not to realize that their one day a year at their old homes was being shortened, their descendants tired of them.

Father tried not to be abroad that afternoon. He did not like to embarrass his friends walking in the daytime with lanterns lit, toward the family graves. They knew he thought that what they were doing was superstitious, and whether they also thought so or not, they had to do what was required by their families. They also did not want to embarrass him. So, sometimes when they met him, they would hold the lanterns behind them, hoping he would not see what they carried.

Neither did we see on those Ting family graves the little piles of paper held down by clods of earth, which symbolized fresh winter clothing and bedding and would be transmuted into those needed garments for the ancestors, nor the ashes left from burning paper money and clothes in front of the spirit door of each grave, nor the half-burned sticks of incense in the stone incense burners. Perhaps they had been there and Dada had not taken us until the evidence should have blown away. But even when we were old enough to go without Dada I do not remember seeing them. Perhaps there were no direct descendants left to do these services for these dead.

The old men of the village and some of the village blades would bring their birds to air in the Ting family cemetery. They would squat on top of the larger mounds and hold the birds in their cages out to the breezes.

There were low stone tables in front of the main graves, tables like the wooden ones at which the families ate on the *k'angs*. These were placed in front of the little gateways into the graves, a foot and a bit high, for the use of the spirits as they came and went.

When Father and Mother had time to take us for a walk we could go to the Ming Dynasty cemetery: the impressive graveyard of an official of that time—1368-1644 A.D. This graveyard was too far for Dada to walk in comfort.

Walking through the wheat fields, the ripening grain, bearded amber stalks, with drooping amber heads, an amber sea rippling in the breeze, catching the sun and sending it back again; walking through the kaoliang fields, tall stalks stripped of leaves until near the bronze bush of grain at the top, so the soya beans could grow between the rows in their luxurious greenness; through millet fields, their heavy saffron heads bent low; through fallow fields, brown ridges waiting for the plow; through fields of winter wheat, the green grasslike plant showing through the old snow in the furrows and drifted against the graves, we walked always in the beauty of an abundant land. The fields were a never ending and ever changing giant patchwork pattern spread over the land, for each man dealt with his strips of land as he had a mind to deal, and his strips did not often lie side by side. And walking through the fields Father's face was the face of a prophet, as he told us stories of the "sower who went forth to sow."

By the sides of the footpaths and the roads and on the grave patches there would be wild flowers in the spring: violets and purple vetch, milkweed with delicate green and yellow cups, little yellow daisies, bluebells, and a purple trumpet with honey at the bottom of the flower which we would suck, and dandelions. The village women, in their blue cotton clothes, came out with their baskets and dug dandelion greens. And later, when the yellow blossoms fluffed into old men's heads, we blew them for the time of day.

Every year the three-hundred-year-old graves in the Ming Dynasty cemetery sank lower and every year they shrank in diameter as the plows of the farmers bit ever closer; for the family had long since died out and there had been none for a hundred years or more to add earth to the graves each year. There were none to defend the dead from the living.

One of the stone lions guarding the entrance had fallen into the sunken road that cut across the corner of the cemetery and lay head down in the bank, but his mate still stood on duty. John and I were proud when we graduated from riding the stone rams and could scramble up onto the stone horses. Mother took photographs of the stone animals and sent them to the missionary societies in America.

The two stone officials, their high stone hats over their upcombed long Ming Dynasty hair, stood gravely ready to counsel their lord, forever ready to raise to their faces the little "audience boards" they held in their clasped hands before their chests, to prove they had no swords hidden up those long wide sleeves and to keep the impurities of the breath from offending their lord. They stood in eternal calm and wisdom.

We loved these walks, John and I.

10

OUTSIDE THE GREAT BACK GATE

PERHAPS MR. CHU, WHEN his family was small, had lived in our compound, but by the time I began to visit them they had a home of their own so near our compound that neither Mother nor Dada thought it necessary to accompany me when I went to see them. In fact, until I crossed their threshold I was still in our compound. I went out the Great Back Gate, and crossed our threshing floor to what had been next door, Mr. Ting's threshing floor.

Although the Ting family next door was still solvent, they rented out the back of their compound, which was laid out exactly like ours. The compounds had been built by brothers. Either they no longer had their money in land and did not need their farm yard and threshing floor, or had leased out all their land and no longer harvested the crops themselves, or they were becoming poor and needed all the income they could get.

Their big farm yard was leased to a dye shop. Over the top of our wall we could see the upper portions of the blue cloth hanging to dry on the high frames made necessary by the long bolts of cloth. We could see the tops of these drying frames and the long poles used by the workmen to handle the cloth, as they hung it up and took it down again. In the spring we could see the workmen crawling along the poles as they bound the framework for another season. Their skill and daring, climbing high and crawling along the poles high in the air, was used by the men of the Dye Shop Guild to hang as "lions," head down when they performed the lion dances during the New Year season or at temple fairs. We got used to the faint odor of indigo that drifted always over the wall. In summer, when the wind blew from the east and they had a new brewing on, the stench, as Mother called it, that came over the wall was almost over-powering to her.

I have never minded the smell. It is even fragrant to me, for it is associated with the house in Huang-hsien and with its deep, rich blue that never washes out, that fades to a more pleasing hue at every washing, that is worn by the people, by all the people.

The neighbor's threshing floor, the same size and in the same relative position as ours, had been leased to Mr. Chu. Now that his dairy was growing and increased his income, added to his salary as Father's teacher, he could afford and needed more space. He had built a house against the north wall, facing south, of course, and stables for the cows against the east wall. There was, of course, a wall between his courtyard and our threshing floor. This was Mr. Chu's first house, where he lived until he was prosperous enough to move to a compound of several courtyards in the middle of the village, where the family used the front gate and the cows lived in the back court and used the back gate. In this first house, however, people and cows used the same gate.

When Father landed in P'eng-lai, a young man of twenty-three, he had been introduced to Mr. Chu, a young man of about the same age, as his tutor. The language schools where, later, young missionaries learned to read and speak Chinese had not yet grown up. Dr. Mateer of the Presbyterian Mission in P'eng-lai had just begun to work on his primer for teaching the Chinese language, a book that was to be used by many new missionaries, diplomats, and a few business men for many years. Father and Mr. Chu were among the young people on whom he tried out the lessons.

Mr. Chu had been one of the brightest boys in the mission school run by Mrs. Crawford in P'eng-lai, the school she had to give up when her husband founded the Gospel Mission and gave Mother the chance to start her school. Mr. Chu had come to the school penniless, all the family property having been smoked away by his father in opium dreams. He was, however, determined to have an education.

When he built his five *chien* house under the north wall of the Ting family threshing floor there were in his family the old man, his father, with the little grey queue, who used to go out each morning, dressed in a long plum-colored gown and a short copper-colored velveteen top coat, to air his bird and return to smoke the afternoon away; his brother, whose weak will was kept stiffened by Mr. Chu's strong one, and who did the actual work of the dairy business, though Mr. Chu himself ran everything;

and there was Mrs. Chu and Ta Pao, "Big Precious," the
eldest son who was four years older than I, and Ching-tzu,
"Capital City," the eldest daughter who was two years
older than I, and the other children who came along, one
a year almost and died almost as fast. Mrs. Chu was asked,
late in life, how many children she had had. Five had
grown to maturity. "I lost track," she said, "so many
died. The Lord gave and the Lord took away. I was acting
as wet nurse for the Lord's children." Mother counted
that Mrs. Chu had had fifteen children.

On rare occasions when Father told us stories of his
life in China they would begin, "When Mr. Chu and I. . . ."
They went together to the villages where there were
Christians, "to strengthen their faith" and to persuade
more people to become Christians. They went to villages
where there were no Christians, if the village would receive
them. Sometimes even the villages where there were
Church members would not receive them.

"Mr. Chu and I went to P'ing-tu to visit Brother Li—
you know he later became Pastor Li. We heard he was
being persecuted for the Gospel's sake and had been
beaten." When they got near the village Mr. Chu said he
would go in and see how things were. He was a Chinese,
though not of their village. In the angry state of mind of
the villagers it was dangerous even for him to go into the
village but not as dangerous as it would have been for
Father with his blue eyes and white skin and the queue
that was not of the right color. Mr. Chu told Father to
wait on the edge of the kao-liang ("giant sorghum") patch
and to go into the patch, in among the tall plants—growing
to the height of six feet and more—and hide if the mob
came out.

No small amount of courage was needed in those days to do what these two young men were doing. Communications, if any at all, were very slow. The Manchu government left people alone for the most part except for taxes. Each village was in many ways a law unto itself. No one inquired too closely about any suspicious event if there were none of the victim's own people to raise an outcry. If both young men had been killed who would there be to say where? And even if such a thing should be taken to the government what could be proven? Nor did the villagers always realize that this was the period of "gunboat diplomacy," when a missionary's life was worth a city. Germany had not yet taken the big and beautiful port of Tsingtao in payment for a missionary killed.

But Mr. Chu relied on his tongue and his ability to *chiang li*, "talk out the logic of the pattern," "to discuss the reasons," "to be reasonable and to find others reasonable." Mr. Chu also relied on the charm of his personality. Still it took great courage to go into that village where the men who had beaten Mr. Li and threatened to kill him if he continued to believe in that foreign way of doing things that taught men to neglect the spirits of their ancestors and taught women to appear in public—to break down the family, they said, the foundation of society.

Perhaps Mr. Chu did not want Father with him as parts of his explanation might not have met with the approval of the straightforward gospel of the love of God and of Jesus that Father taught. Perhaps not. There is no way of telling. But Mr. Chu was a shrewd man.

It also took great courage for Father to sit on a stone, alone, by the side of the road with the *kao-liang* patch behind him. The leaves of the high growing *kao-*

liang were thick and green, a hundred men could have
hidden in that patch. But he was not afraid of an attack
from behind. The surface of events had not been broken
as far as he was concerned. He and the villagers had not
met, there was therefore no relationship between him and
them. In spite of the seething hatred of the outsider, of
the "foreign devils," who were making so much trouble
for them, the villagers had nothing against this young man
personally. There had been no incident which forced
action upon them as with Mr. Li who lived among them,
or might with Mr. Chu who was thrusting himself in to the
situation. The attack would be a frontal attack if there
were one, and I think my father knew this. Any minute,
however, the mob might pour out of the village, and his
language was not yet adequate to talk peace, to talk
harmony. If they came as a mob it would be in hostility:
there would be no time to talk harmony or the logic of
the pattern, for never is a mob reasonable.

"It was a blessed sight to see Mr. Chu and Mr. Li
coming out of the village, with the village headmen accompanying them. Mr. Li's head was covered with dried
blood. He was a horrid sight. He was all scratched and
his queue torn apart. (The signs of a fight or a beating
were not removed until a full settlement had been made.)
But we were welcomed to the village."

Another diplomatic victory for Mr. Chu.

It was typical of the Victorian age and the Chinese
pattern that these two young men, who were close co-
workers for over twenty years and friends for fifty, should
never have called each other by their names but always to
have kept the "Mister" or "Teacher," the same word in
Chinese, between them. Mr. Chu called Father "Teacher"

because he was the pastor and had come to teach the gospel. Father called Mr. Chu "Teacher" because he taught the language and opened for him the classics and the doors into Chinese culture. Anyway it was the custom to address each other by relationship and not by name.

Together the two young men built the church that neither could have built without the other: one with his worldly wisdom and charm and the other with his love of God and man and his gentle patience. And each learned from the other.

It was Father and Mr. Chu who saved the mission from a great mistake.

A new missionary had been sure that he was a very potent force for the Lord. A whole village had sent for him to preach and had responded to his preaching. All in the village wanted to be baptised and join the church. Glowing, he came and told Father the news and wanted to stage a mass baptizing immediately, or at least start the mass enquirers' classes.

"Wait a bit," said Father after the tale poured out. "It does not sound natural. Let's wait and see what's behind it."

"Do you doubt the power of the Lord to convert a whole village at once?"

"No," said Father, "but it very seldom happens that all men think alike about anything at any one time. It can hurt nothing to wait. Have you talked it over with Mr. Chu?"

The young missionary grumbled that Mr. Chu had said the same thing and asked, "Have you talked it over with Mr. Pruitt?"

"I don't like the look of it. That everyone in a village

should believe in the Gospel all at once and after one
preaching only does not stand to reason," said Mr. Chu
when Father talked with him. "I'm sure there's something
behind it."

A few days later Mr. Chu returned, and there was no
mass baptizing to the glory of the young missionary. The
story Mr. Chu had found was not a strange one. In one
form or other it happened in many places, many times,
perhaps not always in as clear-cut a way. Two villages
separated by a field had a feud of long standing. One village claimed the right of way across a field belonging to
the other village. Each year the village owning the field
plowed it up, and each year the men of the other village
came out immediately and walked the path back into
place.

Then the village owning the field heightened the cold
war. After the annual spring plowing they laid a bundle
of fodder and a halter in the field across the place where
they did not want the path to be made. The men of the
other village knew, when they came to walk the path into
being, that they were being told that only mules and
donkeys passed that way. They were being called four-
footed creatures and denied human dignity.

They went to the priest and the whole village joined
the Catholic Church. Then, since they were church
members, the priest went to the magistrate and got the
lawsuit decided in their favor. What more natural than
that the other village should cast about for some other
church to join so they could appeal the judgment, since
foreigners had more power in their courts at that time than
they?

Father kept away from the official structure of the country. "That is their affair. I am a guest in the country and here only to preach the Gospel and not to interfere in their courts and their politics (as many missionaries, especially the Catholics, did). The changes that are needed the people themselves will make, and they will make them when they know about the love of God and the brotherhood of man."

When Father and Mr. Chu went on journeys they had to take with them all the money they might need. That was no small task and attended with risk. No credit system stretched across the country. Certain businesses, such as the medicine business, had branches all over the country, but these were only in the cities and only a select few could use their facilities. Most men had to carry their own cash. There was no paper currency at that time. The usual currency was the copper cash with the square hole in the center that was strung together in double rows, fifty to a section and five hundred to a string. This currency was very heavy.

Each month the donkey that turned the mill in the school courtyard was sent to the bank in the city to bring back a load of money, enough to pay the salaries and wages and buy food for us and the school for a few days. There were the cook, the boy, and Dada to be paid, two teachers for the school and Mr. Chu, and a cook for the school and a man of all work. On ordinary market days the cook took the little accordion-pleated bank book, which slid into its stiff blue cloth cover, to the grain shop that served as a bank and came back with several strings of cash in each end of the canvas bag he hung over his shoulder, one half in front and one behind, as saddle bags are hung.

Sometimes in their journeys Father and Mr. Chu took with them little silver ingots, shaped like crescent moons with a heavy bulge in the middle, worth a tael, a little more than a dollar, each. Silver could be sold anywhere at the daily market rate. But even silver was heavy if the journey was long and they could not carry enough in the only safe place, the stiff close-stitched canvas money belt which each wore around his waist.

One day Mr. Chu came beaming into the dining room. From his long wide sleeves he pulled a long narrow parcel and from inside the breast of his gown he pulled another, a very small one, that he held onto tightly.

Father unwrapped the long parcel. He knew what it was and they were both as pleased as children with a new toy. Father took off the soft Chinese paper in which the parcel was wrapped diagonally and brought out a polished box of redwood. Gently he loosed the copper catch. Every contained movement showed it held something important. In the box lay a tiny pair of scales, the two little copper plates gleaming. He held it up by the red silk cord in the middle of the tiny hard redwood arm and the two plates balanced perfectly. From another section of the box he brought out the tiny weights.

Then Mr. Chu unwrapped the parcel he had been holding—long thin strips of gleaming yellow metal, about five inches long and a third of an inch wide, shining strips of gold.

"One cuts off a piece, weighs it with these scales. . . . It can be sold anywhere. Of course the dealers weigh it with their scales also."

Nothing would do but that they cut off a piece then and there and weigh it, for the joy of using their new toy.

The light from the kerosene lamp hanging over the dining room table shone on their pleased and serious faces, so alike and so different.

Mr. Chu was a fine looking man by any standards. He had a high forehead and a straight nose, large light brown eyes set straight in his head, and the size of his cheeks was in harmony with the width of his forehead. His good teeth were even and his lips were neither too thick nor too thin. He walked with the free easy upright walk of a man of affairs who was yet an educated man. His was the type of face for whose owner the fortune-tellers always fortold high and good destiny.

There was a deep-seated aversion among Chinese to using cow's milk. It was with disgust that they saw foreigners drinking the milk and eating the fat in the form of butter and preserved milk in the form of cheese, ancient and stinking milk. They had no land they could set free for pastures. The land had to raise grain for human beings to eat, but there was also a feeling of something unclean in their attitude toward milk.

Our parents felt it important that we children have milk, and not canned milk only. There was no powdered or evaporated milk in those days. The condensed milk was a thick syrupy substance, very sweet and open to much doubt as to its powers of nourishment. We children liked to spread it on our bread like jam. At first we had our own cow. A teenage boy was engaged to tend the animal, lead her to grass on the grave plots and the sides of the roads, and to see that by no possible chance she ate any of the farmers' grain. She gave about a quart of milk a day and stayed fresh only as long as she would naturally suckle the calf, or perhaps a very little longer.

The calf had to start the milk each time and be pulled away. It became a greater and greater tug-of-war each day between the calf and the milkman.

Mr. Chu discovered that the opium smokers—men who were able to eat very little—could take milk and liked it. He asked for a loan and started a dairy. He sold milk to us and to the opium smokers and made money.

I do not remember Dada taking me to visit the Chu family. Perhaps she did not think it necessary to go with me where all were friends of the family and I did not have to go off mission property. I would try to get Ching-tzu to play with me. Ching-tzu, meaning "Capital City," was so named because she had been born when her father was on a trip to Nanking. It was no small thing to visit either Nanking, the southern capital, or Peking, the northern capital. There were no railways or bus lines in those days, only a few coastal steamers, unless one wanted to spend months going overland and by the Grand Canal. Ching-tzu, however, could not play much. She always had to carry around the next to the last baby while her mother suckled the littlest baby and did the house work.

Ta Pao, "Big Precious," was never at home. He was at school where they called him by his school name, Chu Pao-ch'en, never, of course, by his milk name, his little name, by which we called him. In school he behaved, as he always did, like a dignified old man. Ta Pao was always gentle and dignified. We all loved him. Part of the time he was out with the cows. One day he had spat blood. When Dr. Randall, the new missionary doctor in Ping-tu, came on one of his trips, Mr. Chu asked him for advice.

"Stop keeping him bending all day over books in a stuffy room. Keep him in the air and sunshine. Feed him

eggs and milk." This latter was easy for Mr. Chu. But
how to keep him in the air and sunshine?

"You keep cows. Send him out with the cows each
day."

Send his son, the young scholar and gentleman, out
with the cows like a common day laborer! It was a bitter
idea to Mr. Chu. Also he felt he would lose face, lose caste
among the neighbors, lose part of the position he was
building up so carefully.

"A dead scholar or a live son." Dr. Randall put the
problem neatly and brutally.

So for many months, at least, Ta Pao spent part of
his time holding one end of a rope while the cow on the
other end grazed slowly over a grave plot or the bank by
the side of the road. Ta Pao's lungs never recovered
entirely, but he lived to late middle age and did much good
work in the world as a self-effacing physician, healing
others who were ill.

Mrs. Chu claimed me. "You must teach me English."
A baby a year, all the housework to do until Mr. Chu got
a wife for his brother, and still she wanted to learn
English. So for a period I would go several times a week
to that home beyond our threshing floor.

I would sit solemnly on the six-inch-high threshold of
the common room while Mrs. Chu sat on the round mat
of braided corn husks, her legs folded in front of her, on
the packed earth floor in front of the built-in stove. She
would be feeding pine branches to the fire under the
cast-iron cooking basin or pulling the belows, also built
in, and probably also feeding the last baby. Even more
solemnly I would sit on the *k'ang* in the brief moments
of Mrs. Chu's greatest leisure, while she "studied English"

and nursed the baby and worked on shoe soles. The smell
of wood ashes and pine cones (used as kindling) and of
whole grain cooking hung always in the air. And, as the
Chu family was comfortably well off, a smell of hot fat
lingered like a memory, while over all was the fragrance
of soya sauce. The smells from the cow sheds against the
east wall were aromatic and not too pervasive in the dry
North China air. The latest baby would be at Mrs. Chu's
breast, wrapped in her overlapping coat, that second womb
in which all North China babies were carried, from which
they would push themselves sometime during their second
year as the Chinese reckoned, their first after birth. There
would also be the shoe sole in her hands, that pickup
work of the Chinese housewife of that time, a work of
which there never was an end. She would take a stitch
while repeating the strange sounds I made and glance at
the primer from time to time to see the strange shapes
associated with the sounds.

Perhaps, when I got there, Mrs. Chu would be in the
courtyard making the cloth pasteboard all used in the
soles of the shoes they wore and every woman made for
her family; pasting the scraps of cloth—all left over pieces,
all the bits from worn out clothes—on a plank. After the
pasteboard had dried on the plank leaning against a sunny
wall, she would pull it off and cut it into shoe-sole sizes.
Sewing these lifts together with hempen twine was the
work forever in the hands of every woman. The half-done
shoe soles with the long steel needle stuck in one of the
holes, the small drill and a loop of hempen twine, lay on
every window sill, ready to be picked up when there was
time for a stitch between other duties. The characteristic
double pull of the cobbler, arms spreading outward, made

their wide sleeves into square-rigged sails.

One day when I got there Mrs. Chu was standing at the door of her house. Her coat was open and her trousers had been lowered to show the full great round of her pregnancy. An old woman was examining her carefully, her old eyes close to the skin. Bit by bit she went over the whole surface.

"We are looking," said Mrs. Chu to me without embarassment (nor did I expect any), "to see if the baby will be a boy or a girl."

"It will be a girl," said the old woman straightening up. "See that red line running from between your breasts to your navel?" And in spite of Mrs. Chu's strong desire for a boy, it was a girl.

Mrs. Chu's forehead was high and narrow and there were a few pockmarks on her face. Almost everyone had a few pockmarks. They were fortunate if the whole face was not covered, for everyone had smallpox. The little girls were taught to eat everything in their bowls by being told that every grain of millet or rice left meant a pockmark on the face of the future husband. Mrs. Chu's was a pretty little face and an animated one. She had come from Manchuria but of a family who had emigrated from Shantung Province. Her features looked as though it might have been a scholarly family. Her feet had been bound when she was very small so that unbound they were still little, not much larger than Dada's. Dada made no effort to unbind hers, and she was never able to walk with any but the gait of the bound-footed woman.

When Mr. Chu got a wife for his brother, another widow with a daughter, I had another playmate, subject always to the arrival of another little brother or sister.

Mr. Chu never thought much of his brother's intelligence or of his ability. It was, of course, as the older brother and the moneymaker of the family, his duty to provide his brother with a wife. Widows came cheaper than unmarried girls. He got a widow for his brother. She brought a daughter with her, Elan, just my age. The widow was tall, a well-built country woman with a strong square face. She never said much but she was able to take over the work of directing her husband and providing the will power, so the business flourished even more and Mr. Chu appreciated her, though he never liked his brother.

There was a baby in this room, this branch of the family, only every other year. Elan's mother—we never called her Mrs. Chu, though sometimes we called her Chu Erhsao, Second Elder Sister-in-law Chu—maintained that she carried her babies twelve months before they were born.

When Mr. Chu moved his family to the compound in the middle of the village, I saw less of Ching-tzu and Elan.

All these old playmates of mine were married while I was away at boarding school. Mr. Chu, as all good parents should, arranged their marriages for them, and, as a leading member of the church, of the club, he was able to mate them with the sons and daughters of other and prosperous leading members. Each marriage was another step upward in the social scale. Ta Pao he married to a daughter of the land-wealthy Chang family of the Rear Chang Village of the White Dragon. The girl was counted a beauty. She did not look like her mother. She bore Ta Pao three children and died of tuberculosis. She died cursing him, saying that he had given it to her. By this time Ta Pao had graduated from the newly organized medical school, in its first class, in Wei-hsien, and was a much loved physician in Huang-hsien. We were all happy that the widow he then married was good to him and added to his vigorous family.

Mr. Chu chose for Ching-tzu the smartest boy in Mother's school, who had learned English so well he became English secretary for the Tao-t'ai, the highest civil official in Chefoo. Ching-tzu was quiet and studious, the young man gay and vivacious. He left her with his mother in the old home, with not even a son, and took a concubine in Chefoo. The new missionaries were outraged, and demanded he be divorced. The Chinese were outraged. Who ever heard of a man being divorced. A woman, yes, but a man, never. The battle raged. The new missionaries won. Ching-tzu came home and a new husband was found for her within the church membership, a young teacher, and she, like her mother, bore many children, but not as many as had her mother.

Elan, who was now also one of the Chu family, was married to Fifth Dog, the fifth son of Mrs. Wang of the Wang village outside the East Gate of the Wall of Protection. Fifth Dog had a dignified school name but I do not remember it. We always knew him as Fifth Dog.

Steadily Mr. Chu rose in the world. He learned some Western medicine from the mission doctor, though he left Western medicine mostly to his son. He learned Chinese medicine from the books and from other doctors through the years. He became a well-known healer and favorite in the treatment of the illnesses of the gentry. His second surviving son became a dentist, trained in the school of Western dentistry at Chengtu, in Szechuan Province in the far west. That Mr. Chu could send his son across the country, far to the west, was indication enough of his high financial standing. The young dentist married one of my "little sisters," one of the twins. He did well in a Peking practice. In due time, when his father and Ta Pao had died, he became the head of the family, and saw that his daughters and his nephews and nieces (Ta Pao's children) went to college and entered professions. Among them were a kindergarten teacher, a social worker turned librarian, an oral surgeon, an ophthalmologist, a trained pianist, a professor of economics, and others I have not heard about.

Mr. Chu died in the full knowledge that he had done his work well for his family and for his church, according to the pattern of the time. He lived, his last years, in a spacious compound of many courtyards, surrounded by many descendants.

Ta Pao, whom we all loved, had lived and died in a one courtyard house, next door to the hospital, where he ran the outpatient service and where he was always on call.

11

THE NEIGHBORS COME TO US

OTHER PEOPLE FROM OUTSIDE came to our compound. To the House of the Women came village women, visiting, sightseeing. Sometimes they came brought by Liu Ta-niang, Old Aunt Liu, the village matchmaker, midwife, and commission agent for family women who could not easily go outside their gates, those women who could not leave their gates unless well convoyed. She also added to her income by making paper cash and taels for burning at the graves. The women would come, not as I often saw them as they stood in their doorways, in their everyday blue cotton clothes and with no make-up on their faces, but dressed for the street, for visiting. Their knee length coats of bright colors and better cloth than they wore at home, and the wide ankle length trousers, bound in at the ankle, still showed the creases made when they lay on the shelves of the high wardrobes. Their faces would be white with the thick layers of powder

123

and their cheeks rouged a bright red. Large red circles had been printed across the tips of their lips. Sometimes they would have a small red dot on their foreheads. I thought them very beautiful and stylish looking. No woman went abroad, except the old, without first whitening her face and putting red on her cheeks. It was part of her outdoor costume, as lipstick is to modern woman, as hats and gloves were to the Edwardians.

These women came from our village and they came from Shan Chia, the Shan family village, about three *li* (one mile) away, or any other of the many villages that dotted the fertile Huang-hsien plain, villages that looked, as one walked along the highways, like patches of well-kept woodland.

The women sat around our sitting room as near the doors as possible in the summer to catch the breezes and as far from the stove in winter, for they would be clothed to sit in their own rooms heated only by flues under their *k'angs*. These women had never been to see us before and they never came again. Mother always received them graciously and showed them the house, to see which she knew they had come and hoped it was not the only thing for which they had come.

"Oh, you have your matting on the floor," if it were summer. "Oh, you have your rugs on the floor," if it were winter. In Chinese homes matting and rugs were on the *k'angs*, those brick platform-beds where people sat with their shoes off. The floors in wealthy homes were paved with burnt brick, in ordinary homes with hard packed earth. People could spit in comfort and mothers could clean up easily if the children heeded nature's calls. They could dump a shovel-full of ashes on the spittal or on the child's accident and sweep it all up. No harm would have been done.

"And why do you hang cloth in the windows?" they said. "Doesn't it shut out the light?" They touched the brown flannelette curtains I so disliked. When they wore out Mother gave up curtains. "Dust catchers," she called them.

"Oh, the bed is soft." They pressed down hard on it with their hands. Liu Ta-niang had told them evidently some of the wonders, or horrors, they would see and they wandered from room to room until they found them. "We sleep on hard beds. Of course soft ones are better." It was the formula, the polite formula. It was evident from their faces they knew their beds were better. They were being polite.

"How do you heat them?" they said, lifting the counterpane hanging over the edge of the bed and looking under to see if there were hidden any strange foreign way of heating, since evidently there were no flues under the bed, and since there was no stove attached. "How do you keep warm in winter?" The flues of their cook stoves ran under their k'angs, keeping them warm in winter and dry in summer. In summer they cooked, if possible, only in the mornings.

"Ah, you are like the people of the south, you also keep your night pot in your room." There was the scorn of the Northerner, the people of Han, from the Han Dynasty, for the Southerner and his ways, people who called themselves T'ang people from the T'ang Dynasty, almost four hundred years later. Northerners considered night pots in the house to be unclean, and such customs to show inferior stamina. They themselves always went outdoors, whatever the weather or time of day or night, to the latrine in the corner of the courtyard or behind the house.

Mother would try to get in a few words about the Gospel. Again, obviously, they had been warned. "Oh yes, that is the doctrine. It is good teaching," and they would move on to another room or, if seated, their eyes would glaze over. "Yes, it is a good doctrine but I am only a stupid woman. I have no learning. I cannot understand such things." Then, all the sights seen, they would go away. I wonder how much Liu Ta-niang charged per head.

Liu Ta-niang tried to persuade Mother to put her on the payroll as a Bible woman. She even brought "inquirers"—women who tried to listen to Mother explaining the Gospel without their eyes glazing over. But Mother was not cajoled.

There were statements the visitors always made.

"How white their skins are! It must be because they eat white bread all the time," one of the women calling on Mother said to another. "You see we eat millet and our faces are yellow." This was no more peculiar a deduction for the pre-scientific age than that night air caused malaria or that grape seeds inflamed the appendix.

There were questions they always asked.

"Have you found a mother-in-law for your daughter?" The earlier that important problem of a future home for the daughter was solved, the better the parent.

"Oh," Mother would answer, "We parents don't arrange the marriages in our country, either for our daughters or our sons."

The visiting women would puzzle a moment over this

new idea and then put it gently aside as too difficult for them to understand.

"We make our own marriage decisions," Mother would continue.

"Oh, foreigners have so much ability." This was politeness. Of course, no one in the world had more ability than the Chinese. How could the foreigners operate with so unnatural a pattern? "How could the orderly pattern of life continue if each child chose his or her own mate?" was the question seen in their eyes.

The answer to one of the questions they asked never seemed to satisfy them. "Why did you leave home?" Home was, of course, where my Father's father lived. Why had my father separated himself and his family so far from his father and his brothers and their sons? It was inconceivable to these people that anyone would leave home unless he had to: as an official who had to serve in a province other than his own; as a merchant who took as few outside trips as he could; or, and always this hung in the background, as an exile to pay for some crime against the authorities. Poverty, of course, was another reason: when men went to Manchuria, for instance, to seek their fortune when no living could be made at home. Obviously we had enough to live on and live well by current standards. The explanation that my parents had come to teach the Gospel only somewhat comforted them. "To do good," they would say, "Oh yes, to do good," and the shades of the holy men in the temples would fall over us.

Our callers would feel somewhat at peace for us when they learned there was a mother's sister with five sons—*Ah, liang-i tsu-mei*, "siblings of two sisters"—and were more at peace when they learned there was a mother's-brother uncle. He would see that his sister and her children had fair play. These uncles and aunts lived, of course, in another place than we did. The mammoth distances were not conceivable to these people who had never moved more than ten or twenty miles from their homes.

Some women, Mother's friends, came to visit us from distant villages. They would stay in the guest rooms in the House of Those Who Also Must be Cared For, or in the little house in the Bamboo Court behind the Ancestral Hall. They would come after the wheat harvest was over and before that of the small crops. As it was midsummer, their favorite place to sit and talk with Mother would be the back entry to the sitting room. Ordinary houses had no windows or doors in the back, to the north, for the cold winds of winter came from the north, the evil influences the people feared. Well-built houses had high, narrow horizontal windows on the north that could be opened in summer, to carry off the hot air and give a cross draft, and that could be bricked up in winter. Houses of the wealthy, besides the veranda in front which let in the sun in winter and kept it out in summer, had a passageway across the back, of the same width as the veranda, as an extra shield from the north winds. This had been cut up in our house into a pantry back of the dining room, a dressing room back of the parents' bedroom, and an entry way back of the living room where we hung our coats and hats. With all the doors open there would be a breeze here if there were one anywhere.

Mother's friends would sit on the doorstep, on mats on the floor, on stools. They would fan themselves and talk and talk. Mother would knit. Her friends said she knitted in her sleep. Never could she sit with hands idle. Sometimes she would prepare the fruit for canning, pitting the cherries, peeling the peaches and apples that we would eat the next winter. She would sit in her long black alpaca skirt and knee length white grass linen upper garment with the wide shoulder length yoke and eight inch border of deep-blue grass linen on the foot-wide sleeves, her hair combed back into a chignon at her neck, looking as much like a Chinese woman as she could manage. Her brown hair and eyes helped, but her nose always gave her away.

Among those who sat most often with Mother were Mrs. Kao, Mrs. Chiang, and Mrs. Chang. They would talk for hours about things that bored me. When they came I would not stay around, but, having greeted them, would go away and play. They would talk for hours, and they talked about how good was the Lord and told each other their troubles.

Mrs. Kao was a plain little woman with bright sharp eyes and prominent gums. I always looked at her hair, combed carefully back into the hard chignon just above her collar, and wondered how her husband took hold of it to pull her around as I had heard the parents say he did, and all because she refused to worship his ancestors. "But," Mother would say, "her Christian conduct and patience won out." He later joined the church himself, and their son, much later, became a Christian pastor. Mrs. Kao lived a long day's journey by donkey back from us and so stayed several days each time she came.

Mrs. Chiang was not five feet tall (unusually small among the big Shantung men and women). Her husband was a leper and a small farmer. Her will was as large as her body was small. There was a story of her having been caught in a flooding river on a furry little donkey, and the Lord's having saved her in answer to her prayers. After that she promptly devoted her life to trying to save the souls of others. Floods came down so fast in the summer that a man rolling up his trousers to wade a tiny stream would sometimes meet a river before he had crossed half the wide sandy stretch between the two lines of trees bordering the banks.

Mrs. Chang came from Hou Pai Lung Chang Chia, the the Chang Family of the Rear White Dragon Village. The Chang family was one of the few wealthy families in the church connection. They had possessions of lands and houses. I used to wonder why so few rich families joined the church; and then I wondered why any did. Most of the wealthy families of Huang-hsien were anti-foreign and deeply set in their ways, in their worship of their ancestors, and sure of themselves and their culture that had served their people so many hundreds and even thousands of years. The doubt that had begun to corrode in the intellectual circles in the great cities had not yet reached them. They did not like the strange foreign ways and they had no need of food, which was the reason for some to join the church.

Mrs. Chang had a huge jutting nose, a thing most uncommon among the Chinese and not admired. Her hair, in spite of all the tree bark fluid and combed-back restraint, showed a tight wave that would have done credit to any modern beauty parlor. This also was most uncommon among Chinese and considered, at that time, most unbeautiful. Her hair and nose were such as are seen in some T'ang Dynasty paintings and on the clay figures of at-

tendants placed in the T'ang Dynasty tombs, the dynasty
when foreigners, people from the vast reaches of Central
Asia and across Asia Minor, came to the great and rich
country of Cathay. Mrs. Chang was also known as one
with a bad temper. Had she quarrelled with all her relatives and neighbors? Did she find a social life in this
new club that she was denied elsewhere? Did her mind
reach out like her jutting nose? Perhaps she was gropingly
seeking God, seeking goodness, as so many of the church
members undoubtedly were, and learning new definitions.

She came in her smart sedan cart, every bit of the
latticed wooden top, the wheels, and shafts, polished, the
brass and copper fixtures shining. The well-tailored blue
cloth cover was handsomely decorated with black bindings
and appliqué. Mrs. Chang was old enough to sit in the
front of the cart with the curtain up and enjoy seeing
what was going on. She did not need to depend on the
little pane of glass let into the front curtain, which was
beginning to displace the little square of patterned silk
gauze. Mother enjoyed her visits. Mrs. Chang had a mind.
But Mother did not enjoy her visits as much as she did Mrs.
Kao's. Mrs. Kao had a heart as well a mind.

There were men who came to see Father. He received
them in his study in the Master's House. I did not see
much of them until I was eight years old, when desks were
set in the study for John and me so that we might have
regular lessons (we already knew how to read and write)
and do our sums under Father's guidance, while Mother
taught in the Boys' School.

The church members, most of whom were farmers
with strong broad faces and clothes of thick coarse
homespun cotton dyed blue with indigo, came to Father

with their problems and to pay their respects when they came to the *hsien* city (their market town) on business. They would sit squarely on the edge of their chairs and talk with their harsh East Shantung voices, with the flat East Shantung accent. They came also at New Year time to give their New Year greetings, to wish Father happiness and wealth and to congratulate him on another year added to his age. And he would do the same to them.

Everyone in the country added a year to his age at New Year and not on his birthday as we do. So we always had two ages, our Chinese age and our American age. As I was born late in December and the Chinese New Year came in February, two months after I was born, I was two years old when I was two months old. For most of the year I had to give my Chinese age as two years older than my American age.

I thought then that it was a strange custom—reflecting the thinking, as I was, of the Westerners around me. Was not one's age something very personal? Not until many many years had passed over me did I realize the wisdom that could think in terms of all the people. Birthdays were very special, personal days, and celebrated for the old and the honorable who had earned the right to such distinction. In so universal a thing as age, however, all progressed together.

Dressed in their formal robes of faded blue cotton, newly washed, these farmers clumped in to see Father in their heavy shoes with the big flat nails in the soles. Mr. Chu and Dr. Fan and a few of the gentry would come too. Dressed in their long blue or plum-colored silk formal robes, with their formal hats on their heads, they were as beautiful in their way as the farmers in theirs. A faint scent of sandalwood with which the formal robes had been stored hung around the gentry, a faint scent of indigo in which their robes had been dyed hung around the farmers.

They all had two things in common, no matter how different their stations in life. They all wore ceremonial robes cut in the same pattern, no matter what the material, and they all had dignity, a dignity and integrity in their bearing, in their every movement, and in the expressions on their faces, the dignity and integrity that belonged to all in the same way that New Year belonged to all.

They came into the room, they bowed to my father and accepted his bows, as men who knew their own worth, the worth of their way of life, their pattern of living, as men who knew they were human beings and therefore of consequence, and who were doing the right thing. They had been brought up to know what was right, had *ch'eng jen*, "become adult" and mature human beings who knew that all responsibilities had their privileges and all privileges their corresponding responsibilities. They knew the intricate pattern of life, the relationships between human beings, between human beings and the soil on which they lived, and between human beings and the ancestors who had passed to the world beyond. They tried to order their lives so that all elements inside them and around them harmonized. The wise among them, as I came to know, sought always to find ever deeper meanings in the pattern; those who were not wise but were good tried to follow the pattern as it was taught; and those who rebelled were called unfilial by all but the wise. All, however, knew that all life was a rhythmic process of ever interacting *yin* and *yang*, of opposites forever interacting and acting on each other.

12

THE JAPANESE WAR: 1894-1895

ONE YEAR OUR COMPOUND housed many refugees. Strange men came to see Father one day in the winter of 1894-1895. As it was the day after Chinese New Year I thought they had come to give New Year greetings to Father, but they did not look like New Year callers. They did not have on ceremonial garments and snow was melting on their thick padded plue or black cotton clothes. Their faces were dark and grooved, the flesh clinging to the bones from cold and anxiety. The Japanese, they said, had shelled P'eng-lai. There were Japanese warships lying off the shore. The Japanese, they were sure, were about to land and sack the city. A shell had fallen in Miss Moon's compound. Miss Moon was a venerable American missionary in P'eng-lai. A shell had cut a man in two.

Those who could leave the city were fleeing: those who had places to go. The members of the P'eng-lai church were on their way to Huang-hsien. These men were the advance messengers. Would the brethren of the Huang-hsien church give them refuge?

P'eng-lai was sixty *li* (twenty miles) away. These men had pushed through the deep snow and high wind. The others would be an hour, two hours, three hours later. School was out for the winter holidays. Could they live in the school quarters? Could they come in to the church?

The people of Huang-hsien became worried. P'eng-lai was only sixty *li* away. Strong men could walk it in six hours. Our city lay between P'eng-lai and the capital of the province, on the main highway. What if the Japanese marched to the capital, burning, looting, raping as they went? Why should the people not worry? Everyone in the district, everyone in the country had been brought up on tales of the T'ai-p'ing wars, of the devastation made by the Long Haired Ones. Were there not two walls around our city? Were not many villages in our plain surrounded by mud walls that were cumbling over the years? Walls kept out marauders armed with spears, they kept out those armed only with bows and arrows or even with muskets, but would they keep out shells? P'eng-lai had a wall. Would the Japanese haul their heavy guns over the winter roads? Would the walls of the city and of the villages and the high walls of our compound which had protected the Ting family from the T'ai-p'ings protect the people and the members of the two churches from the Japanese?

These were barbarian invaders, not their own people, barbarians from the borders of the Empire, from the Eastern Sea, from where the sun rises. They were barbarians who had rebelled, the people said, from the Middle Kingdom, from the rule of the Emperor, the Son of

Heaven, in Peking. No one knew what the invaders would do, but whatever invaders did was bad. "Conquering as they go, they burn and loot. They kill the old and the young. They take the young men for work and the young women for pleasure." This was the formula, learned from millennia of disasters.

Even more than the invaders the people feared their own soldiers, should they be defeated and, dispersed, flee over the land. "Defeated soliders. . . . Soldiers fleeing. . . . If the garrison in P'eng-lai is defeated. . . . If the defeated soldiers flee before the Japanese. . . ." Defeated soldiers knew no laws of conduct—only of survival. This was another set of formulas old as the race.

The people from P'eng-lai began to arrive: first the men, but even they did not come as fast as the tales of hardship, of travel in the deep snow, of women giving birth in caves dug in the snow. Perhaps there were women who gave birth in snow caves. There would always be women near their time and it was not strange that the sentence, "And the women gave birth in the snow caves," should become a formula for flight in the winter. But there were no new babies among those who came to our compound and lived in the school quarters: the men and women and children who had walked the sixty *li* through snow two feet deep. The Japanese had shelled P'eng-lai on the day before Chinese New Year.

Rumors flew as thick as snowflakes. The people of Huang-hsien watched Father closely. If he had shown any signs of leaving there would have been panic and the people would have streamed across the countryside, fleeing to any place they could find. People would have been sure that he had secret word from the American consul in Chefoo that the Japanese were coming.

The rich Ting men from across the street and from next door came and begged Father to store boxes of their valuables in our compound. Dressed in their long fur-lined silk robes they came and bowed to Father, whom never before they had even acknowledged to be there. Where we lived, the land we lived on, according to treaty, was a bit of America, or at least had American protection, it was argued. The Japanese, our neighbors and the church members reasoned, would not want to become embroiled with America and so would leave us and all with us, alone. This was the period of "gunboat diplomacy," when the life of a missionary (whether he wanted it to be so con-sidered or not) was worth a province, or at least a treaty port, to the Western Powers.

But there was no American flag in the compound. It was decided to make two, one to hang at the Front Gate and one to hang at the Back Gate. For days the refugee women sat on the green grass and red roses of the "Brussels carpet" in the living room and sewed together strips of red and white cloth. Other women cut out and fitted the white stars on the blue field. Even with the help of the dictionary no one was quite sure how many stars there should be.

To the great thankfulness of all the flags were never used. The Japanese did not land in P'eng-lai and did not come overland. They fired a few shells—three or four at most—to divert attention from Weihaiwei, further east, at the end of the promontory, which they had intended all along to take, and which they did take.

Father and Mother were pleased they had not needed to use the flags. They were glad the Japanese had not come to trouble the people. They were also glad not to use the alien flags in a country that was not their own. Father consistently refused to mix in the lawsuits in the Chinese courts as did some missionaries, especially the Roman Catholics. He would talk their troubles over with the church members, talk with them as their pastor and their friend, but he would not—a foreigner—meddle in the machinery of their government. He would not use extraterritoriality to build up the church. The justification for using the flag this time, should it have been needed, and a justification arrived at after days of pressure from the Chinese both inside and outside of the church and of careful thought on his part, was that the Japanese were a foreign foe invading China, and that he—another foreigner—might therefore use such means as he could to protect whomever he could. Never was an American flag flown outside the compound gates. Inside the compound the flags could be flown, especially on the Fourth of July. My parents conducted themselves as they would have as guests in any foreign country.

But we children enjoyed the flag making and we enjoyed the refugees, the extra number of people in the compound during the holiday season when compound life was very quiet.

Best of all was the family of the P'eng-lai milkman. They had taken over the three *chien* suite that Dada and her family had once occupied in the southwest corner of the school courtyard. One of the girls was about my age. As she and her elder sister had to sew, I also learned to sew that winter.

One day we, Mrs. Chao, the milkman's wife, my friend Lily and I, and her elder sister Moth, were sitting on low wooden stools around the doorway, for it was a warm day in late winter. Suddenly Moth jumped up and almost pushed me over as she rushed toward the threshold where her mother was sitting. She ran across the common room, into the inner room, and dropped the door curtain. I looked up in surprise from my sewing to see what had frightened her. No one else seemed perturbed. They went placidly on with their sewing. She could not have been concerned. The only change in the scene before us, the only new feature that I could see, was our "boy" stepping over the threshold of the gate leading from our living quarters into the school courtyard, and he was a common enough sight. He was dressed in the more formal clothes for going out, not those in which he worked. He had a long blue gown over the short blue jacket and long blue trousers in which we usually saw him, and a smart black vest over the gown. He was carrying his bird in its cage, taking it out for an airing. I did notice, however, there was a swing to his body and a cock to his head I had never seen before.

I asked a question or two and got nothing but polite "Ah's" in reply. I had learned even then not to press questions but to wait and watch, or ask Mother. The "boy," it seemed, had fallen in love with pretty little Moth. She was only sixteen by Chinese count so could have passed fifteen birthdays only. Pretty she was, with her oval face and her slightly, very slightly bowed nose and fair complexion. Nor was she adverse to him, to the way he looked. The families had bargained and made the contract. The contract once made, Moth could not let her betrothed see her. She had to pretend they had never seen each other. Moth had to run if he appeared, run and hide. I remembered later, in thinking it over, that she had made quite a point of jumping up and overturning the stool she was sitting on, and that she had not run too quickly, though the motions of running had all been there. She must, I thought to myself, have wanted him to see her, really.

It did not seem sensible to the family to take her back to P'eng-lai while the marriage plans went forward, since she would have to come again so soon to be married. Arrangements were made, therefore, for her, her mother and sister to stay on in Huang-hsien, while the milkman, her father, went back to P'eng-lai to care for his cows. He had, by this time, been back in P'eng-lai for some time and all the other refugees had gone back home. To have found a good mother-in-law for one of the daughters was no small thing.

To watch the trousseau being made was fun. For the wedding itself the bride and her family moved out to the home of one of the church members in another village, so she could be taken a fair distance in her red chair. It was the groom's home, therefore, I watched being prepared to receive the bride, and the groom I saw being dressed.

The groom's men, his friends, were helping him. He stood arrogant in his maleness, his long blue silk trousers falling full from his flat hips and gathered into the black satin boots tight on his feet. One of his friends, his groom's men, was giving his queue the last bit of attention as it hung straight and heavy down his back, and the other was adjusting his red silk ash. It was a tightly woven silk sash, very stiff, about three inches wide and many yards long. They wound it around and around him and then adjusted it in front, right down the middle of the front. Arrogantly intent was the groom in all the pride of his manhood, and earnestly intent were his two friends adjusting the sash hanging down in front, and thinking of the time when it would be removed and of that of which it was the symbol.

Magnificent he was that day.

Years later, as I passed through Huang-hsien in a bus which stopped at the bus station not far from my old home, I saw an old farmer standing by, watching. He was not as old as he looked, I could see while the bus tarried, but like one whom life had beaten, or almost beaten, one who carried on because life itself was routine. He did not recognize the foreign woman sitting in the bus as the little girl who had been such a nuisance to him so many years ago, but I recognized him. He seemed to have shrunk and to look more like the old cook, his father, without the old man's fussy importance. He was patient without Dada's strength of purposeful patience.

13

THE PEOPLE OF OUR VILLAGE

WHEN DADA AND HER family moved to a house of their own in the village our world expanded and our appetites unaccountably improved—John's and mine, unaccountably to Mother, or so we thought. While Dada and her family lived in the rooms in the southwest corner of the Farm Court in our compound it had been easy to visit her.

I would follow her home and watch her prepare the evening meal. Wen-tzu, her daughter, would be sitting on the round thick mat of braided corn shucks in front of the masonry stove, feeding the fire under the big stationary iron cooking basin, the millet gruel slowly bubbling in the lower half. I would watch Dada mix the meal—corn and millet and soya bean ground together, shape the loaves in her hands, pat them between her palms until they were about six inches long and four across and about two inches thick. The grooves made by her fingers would be cooked

142

into the loaves. Little puffs of steam would rise as she slapped each loaf against the hot iron. They made a girdle of golden medallions around the top of the cooking basin. The rush of warm steam as she scooped out the millet gruel or detached each golden loaf from the sides of the cooking basin was *hsiang*, fragrant. The warm thick steamed bread was something to chew on; the crust, where the bread had been stuck and held on to the sides of the basin, was crisp and crunchy. I could bite on the soya beans cooked into the millet gruel and on the chips of salt vegetable that I lifted from the center dish and placed on the edge of the gruel. Dada's salt vegetable was of superior flavor. She made it herself, as did all good housewives, in a big jar (almost as tall as I) standing outside her door. That jar balanced the water jar standing outside the door on the other side. Into the salt brine Dada would put any odd piece of vegetable she did not otherwise need. When she wanted a piece of salt vegetable for supper she would dig into the thick brine with her long wooden ladle and fish out a piece from the bottom, a well cured piece, cut it carefully into tiny strips for the family to pick up with chopsticks and eat with the gruel, to flavor the gruel. She would never let us eat the raw scallions and turnips her family crunched so happily. She knew we were not allowed to eat raw vegetables. I would watch her son, the washman, home for his evening meal, break off a hunk of the warm steamed bread, wrap a long green scallion leaf, a foot long, around it and crunch it between his strong white teeth, an expression of bliss creeping over his face.

Chiang Wen-chi, the old cook, showed Father and Mother the deeds to the land he had leased and to the house. There were big square official seals on the soft thick paper. The imprints were red and the characters stylized. The lease was to last for sixty years. I do not know how many years it had taken the three of them to save enough from their monthly wages to accomplish this or how many sharp bargains had helped. Perhaps they had borrowed a little from Father also. Mr. Chu and Chiang Wen-chi were fortunate to be able to borrow from Father. Rates of interest from the userers were high and compounded each month. Once in debt it was a rare man who was able to pay up, who was not ruined.

Chiang Wen-chi was going to be a farmer, and a cook no longer. This was a rise of a step in the social scale. *Shih, nung, kung, shang*—"scholar, farmer, craftsman, merchant." He was moving from craftsman to farmer. He cocked his head to one side like an old bird and showed the deeds. There were several strips of land, most of them north of the village but some west. None, however, would, mean too far to walk when he and his sons went out to plow and sow and reap.

The house he had leased was in the middle of the village where those who farmed their own land or kept shops lived, where the street was not paved as it was in our end of the village, and the gates into the compounds were not wide like ours and those of the wealthy Tings, but not unpainted and sagging like those in the lower end of the village street where the poor lived, those who had no land. The new home was back of the open space in the middle of the village where those who had no threshing floor of their own could thresh their grain, and where the stage was put up when the village elders arranged for one of the traveling companies to perform a singing drama for some religious festival or to pray for rain. There were no dramas performed during the years we were in the village. The increasing poverty of the Ting families still left at the upper end of the village was perhaps one of the reasons, but the one most often given by the village elders was the refusal of the church members to pay the informal tax they levied, on the grounds of its being wrong to worship heathen gods. This did not increase our popularity.

On this open space, during the New Year holidays, dog and monkey shows performed; in the long summer evenings storytellers would entertain the villagers. Someone would bring out a table on which a pot of tea (the tea to be drunk through the spout) would be put, for storytelling dries the throat. The storyteller would lay his fan on the table after he had slapped it shut to emphasize a point. The people brought out backless benches and sat around a hollow square while some stood behind. The storytellers did not come often, however, for ours was a small village.

On warm autumn days the village women would bring the big *kao-liang* straw mats, the kind they spread on their *k'angs*, lay them on the threshing floor and spread their work around them. The winter clothes, which had been taken apart and washed, would be put together again with new cotton padding added. The women would make it a social occasion. And in the lee of the sunny wall the old men would squat for hours, sometimes slowly gossiping, a word here and a word there, or they would just squat and enjoy the sunshine.

Sometimes as we walked down the street we could see three or four or five men squatting in a tight circle and we would know a talk to "achieve harmony" was going on. One of the village peacemakers had been agreed upon as the one to help settle the problem and the case was being explained, detail by detail, by both sides, in the presence of the *shuo ho ti*, of "he-who-talks-harmony." They would talk for hours and sometimes days until each had had his full say and they had all come to an agreement. No one was bound to accept the services of the peacemaker but all knew it was wise to do so, as he was a man of experience and proven wisdom, often also of authority, the authority of age, or education, or of possessions. Sometimes he was a villager of small possessions but large wisdom. That a lawsuit was won only by the mandarin was a common saying. He got the money from both sides, often all their money. Father was sometimes asked to act as the "one-who-talked-harmony" for the church members.

If we asked Dada, "What are they talking about?" she would murmur, "Something important."

If we said, "What important things?" she would say, "Uhhh—"

If we were out walking with Father and Mother we would more likely get an answer. Father might say, "They are probably talking about that boundary dispute. I see Brother Han is one of them." Or he might say, "Stone-mason Liu is one of them—perhaps they are talking about the bonuses he gave his journeymen at the last festival. Some say he was not fair to them—did not dispense a fair share of his profits."

Or Mother might say, "Old Mrs. Wang seems to have been beating her daughter-in-law again. I see the young woman's brother has come from their home village and the Second Wang boy is there." I would ask no more questions, for I knew that in such disputes the men of the families would represent their women, the son would represent his mother, and the young woman's brother would represent her. It was his lifelong duty to protect her and her children.

In Dada's new compound was a house of three *chien* facing south onto a little courtyard. It must have been the office for the village elders, now no longer needed. Chiang Wen-chi had been allowed to encroach on the village threshing floor, to build a little two *chien* house and enclose a small court. When the corn was shucked in the autumn and dried on this flat roof, the house seemed to be roofed with gold. In the warm autumn sunlight Dada and John and I and Dada's second son sat on the roof and shelled the corn, golden kernels flowing through our fingers.

Dada's younger son showed us the big black smuts which grew on the cornstalks. Some of them were good to eat, he said. He also liked to eat the fat grubs he found when he broke open a fresh green cornstalk. John ate them also and said they were good. Although I knew the Swiss Family Robinson had eaten such things, I would not eat them.

We were now seeing more of the village, since Dada moved, and our universe was a larger one. Dada took us to visit in the Ting compound across the street from ours. The eldest Ting daughter was about to be married and the maids were working on her trousseau. As the day was hot they had placed a table in the *chien* left open as a passageway between the Entrance Court and the Master's Garden, where a cool breeze always blew. The maids (middle aged women and Dada's friends) were cutting out garments on the square table they had brought out or were sitting around on benches against the walls, sewing.

Mrs. Ting came out to see the work, looked at a seam or two, at the lines of the garments being cut, and went away again. She was a small thin woman on the further side of forty, with a narrow highbred face. She did not appear to see the strange little girl sitting on the bench with Dada. She knew, of course, of our existence, but like many of the villagers she ignored what she did not like and could do nothing about.

"How many girls are there in the family now?" Everyone knew the answer but it was something to say in the lazy heat.

"Five," said the youngest maid. "This is the trousseau of the Eldest Young Mistress, she's eighteen."

"You forget the real eldest died when she was fifteen. She spat blood."

"Then there were the two who died when they were babies." This was said by the oldest maid to show how long she had been with the family.

"And all of them girls. You should have seen the Old Dowager's face when she was shown each new baby—black as a *yao-kuei*, 'a demon in the temple.'"

"It's a wonder they did not long ago get a concubine."

"Hum. The Old Mistress talked of it each time a baby came, and each time talked longer and louder, but the Mistress was not willing. 'I'm still young,' she would say. 'Let me try again.'"

"If this last baby hadn't been a boy she would have had to put up with a concubine."

"Yes, she had promised the Old Mistress. But the Old Heavenly Grandfather had pity on her. You don't know how much incense that woman has burned."

"It was in her eight characters—in her destiny—that she would have a son."

"Yes, but it could have been through a concubine." All knew this was true and all fell silent, thinking how near the mistress had come to having the nuisance of a concubine cluttering her life, to sharing her home and her husband with yet another woman in the house, and to having her son enter life through the red gate of another woman's body.

The wet nurse, whose whole time was devoted to the precious boy, had joined the party and was sitting on one of the benches, giving suck. She was a big country woman with round healthy cheeks bursting red. The child on her lap was about a year old and lay kicking as he sucked, his feet in little red embroidered shoes.

"But there's something wrong with the Little Master," one of the women said. "The mistress is worried, though most people say it does not matter."

All looked at the little figure lying happily on the wet nurse's lap, at his head pillowed on the wide-sleeved arm. His head, like that of all babies, was close shaven, and like most babies there was an unshaved patch. Whereas with most babies this patch was over the fontanelle, his was on one side. It was peach shaped, the symbol of long life and fertility. The hair was braided with a red cord to decorate it and fasten it.

"How many times a day do you pull the braid?" One of the maids asked the wet nurse. "Really you should pull it gently whenever he is asleep, keep up a steady pull, so 'it' will gradually come into place."

"It would be strange," said the wet nurse, "if I were allowed to touch those few hairs. That is the grand-

mother's own privilege. She won't let anyone else touch
the braid. Even combs it herself."

The women let out their breaths and nodded.

"It's lacking on only one side?" This was asked by a
woman from another village, for whose benefit the maids
had been saying these things they all knew. This woman
was a "wise woman" and had been specially asked to give
her opinion. That the mistress did not know she had been
invited and might never know her opinion, did not matter.
There was probably no more anyone could do anyway
than the braid and the daily pulls on it, unless perhaps to
suggest some potent number of times it might be pulled
in a day, or some temple formula.

The wet nurse took the little boy to the table. He
was dressed like any village baby in nothing but the little
triangular red apron that stretched from chest to bellow
his crotch, covering his stomach, that part of the anatomy
most sensitive to the sudden shifts in temperature. His
apron, however, was of silk.

The wet nurse stood him on the table and swept the
apron up with her hand.

The women gathered around.

"Ah—," said the wise woman peering, "there is one
in place. It is of good shape and firm," said she feeling
gently. "Too bad the pouch on the other side is empty.
But one is enough. He will be able to continue the line
and provide descendants. Tell your mistress that she need
not worry. What a pretty little birdie he has too—looked
at from this side. A pity it's not symmetrical."

Near the center of the village, where the prosperous but not the wealthy lived, almost opposite Dada's
new home, was the compound where lived a retired shoe

manager. He spent much of his time sitting on the threshold of his gate, watching what passed. He was deaf and could not have heard us greeting him had we done so, but Dada told us to pay no attention to him. When he saw us coming his face would become as stony as one of the mandarins in the Ming Dynasty cemetery. Even his iron grey beard, which was not as sparse as most Chinese beards, would seem to turn to stone. And his eyes would be fixed on a spot over the tops of the houses across the street. He hated the people from over the ocean who had invaded his village.

He was a fine looking old man with a high forehead and a strong square face, a bit longer than wide. His was the kind of face that made old women prophesy great things for the one who possessed it, the shape of face most liked in men.

One day Dada took us to that compound. The old man was not sitting on the threshold blocking the way. I need not have trembled even a little, fearing his anger as we invaded his home. I should have trusted Dada. He was away for the day amd his wife had sent for us. She wanted to see with her own eyes what those horrid "ocean people, foreign devils," were like. It was as well to start with a child.

Dada and I went down the gate passage, at the side of the front row of houses, a half *chien* wide, as was fitting in this middle class compound, across the courtyard, to the room of the deaf man's wife. That she was the head of the household could be seen since the two or three other women stood in her presence. They were probably daughters-in-law. She and her guests were the only ones who sat.

The rooms were well furnished. Not only was the mat on the *k'ang* of finely woven strands of *kao-liang* stalk but the pattern was more than usually intricate. On either end of the *k'ang* were many quilts piled high, clean and covered with red or blue silk or fine cotton. The wood of the low table on the *k'ang*, of the bureau against the wall near the *k'ang*, and of the high wardrobe against the north wall, was either hard redwood or covered with fine Ningpo lacquer. There were several chairs set against the walls, straight-backed redwood chairs with flat satin cushions.

The mistress herself I had never seen before. She was never on the street. When she went abroad it was in a sedan cart that she entered from her own farm court at the back, the north end of her compound. Nor was I familiar with her kind of feature. She had the fine drawn face, long and narrow. The nose had a slight suggestion of an aquiline bridge, not like the flat round faces of the women who came to church or whom I saw sitting on the mats making quilts, nor yet like those with the high jutting cheek bones and the well defined jaw lines like Dada. The only other face I had seen like hers was that of Mrs. Ting who lived across the street from us. Neither of these faces was lacking in strength.

Our hostess was very vivacious. Through a continuous stream of chatter she found out all she wanted to know about our family and me that Dada was willing to tell. She looked her fill on the white skin, the strange green eyes, and the pale hair she had heard about. Not much of my hair, however, was showing since Mother kept it cropped as short to the head as was my brother's: not even a bang was left. This had further confirmed me in the opinion that I was a plain little girl.

"They don't shave the head." Our hostess meant the inch back from the hair line all around that little girls' heads were shaved, as well as those of men, until the girls reached puberty. "Hmm. A little oil would keep that hair smoother." My hair must have been a little longer than usual.

"It's not the fashion among the ocean people to put oil on their hair." Dada was holding up our end, although I am sure that she too felt my hair would have been better smooth and shiny. "Ahh." And then, "She wears our coarse cloth in her clothes but cut in a strange way," as she fingered the blue peasant cloth, stenciled with a little pattern of white dots arranged in clusters, of which my dress was made.

Even then I knew the cloth was beautiful but I hated it because my dresses were always made of it, always the same. Jane, who lived in P'eng-lai with her missionary father and mother, had pretty dresses. When she outgrew the dresses sometimes her mother gave them to me. Lately she had sent me a red one with pomegranates and peonies cross-stitched in white around the collar, sleeves and hem. I wished I had the red dress on that day. It was Jane who had asked me, "Do you think in Chinese or English?" I had had to stop and think. I had never before considered the matter. I thought about things and I dreamed about things. I was surprised when I realized that I thought and dreamed in Chinese. After that sometimes it was in one language and sometimes in the other.

Then the Old Mistress turned back my skirt. "Ahh, she does wear trousers."

"Yes, they wear trousers, short ones, not long ones like ours." Dada felt called on to explain.

But I was used to it. The women always turned back my skirt to see if I had on any trousers. Their own were always evident even under the skirts of formal wear (the only time they wore skirts). Their trousers were long and came to their ankles.

The water pipe was brought out by one of the younger women, and offered politely to me as well as to Dada. None of the church people smoked water pipes. I watched fascinated as the little round pellets of tobacco were rolled and placed in the tiny bowl and lit from the paper spill that had to be blown into flame each time it was used, with a few sharp explosive puffs. A couple of gurgling draws and then the pellet was blown out of the tube and the process begun all over again. It seemed to me a lot of work for one small moment of smoke. I did not then realize that much of the pleasure of smoking is in the occupation for hand and mouth.

I wondered if the old man who sat so often in the gateway was the one who had demanded so large a bride price for his sixteen-year-old daughter, so recently dead, that the match had fallen through. I was sorry for the poor dead girl who had to be buried in an unmarked grave, soon to be plowed over, in her father's wheat field, and to have no one to feed her and clothe her in the other world. She might have been buried as a wife, as a matron, in a family graveyard, beside her husband, but for her father's greediness, demanding so large a bride price. The match with the teenage boy, who also was already dead, the son of a wealthy family in another village, had all but been settled. Another dead girl whose parents were more reasonable had been chosen. In due time the dead boy's parents would find a baby, a boy, who would be adopted as the son of the dead couple, who would grow up in the family and care for the old people and for the rites at the graves, whose name would be in the family archives, kept in the family temple. The line of succession would be secured.

One day Dada took us north on the short village crossroad to the village pond. Every city, every village, I was to learn, was planned on a pattern. The two main streets crossed at the center. The Chinese called this the ten ideograph, as that ideograph is in the shape of a cross. Vestiges of this pattern could be found even in villages clinging to the banks of a river or in a mountain valley. In cities and villages on the plains, this pattern was clear. Our village had really only one street, to the east and west. The crossroad to the south was only a footpath between the Ting compound's large garden and the village truck garden. After passing the gardens the path meandered across the fields to an empty, solitary house and on to the East Gate of the Wall of Protection. This house was a deserted family temple, half of whose roof had fallen in. We called it the Beggar's Palace because three or four ragged sick-looking men sheltered there at night and begged in the city by day. The crossroad to the north was only as long as the deaf man's compound but was a village street, for all that. A few dilapidated gates opened onto this street. We could see into the small, bare courtyards that had no spirit screens to guard their bareness.

Lying on the bank of the pond, face down and very still, was the body of a man—the village idiot. He had lived with his mother in one of those little courts. Several of the villagers were standing around looking at him. His wet brown body glistened on the sticky glistening mud and the long tendrils of the weeping willow cast moving shadows over him.

"He had a fit and fell in."

"Perhaps." There was no condemnation for whatever it was that had happened. "Bitter destiny" covered all—his fate and his mother's.

No one was much concerned. He had not been worth much to anyone—not even to his mother who worked as a seamstress to feed him and herself. She came while we were there. She stood on the edge of the pond where he lay, his feet in the water, and looked at him.

Dada drew us away.

Where the roads crossed in our village, near the northwest corner, was the village temple: a little room of about six feet wide and eight deep, set waist high to a man, on a platform of burnt brick, so the gods inside would be on a level above the people and the incense could be offered upward. The doors, as we went by, were usually closed. When they were open John and I would hang onto the ledge and peep in. We never had time to count the gods or look at them carefully before Dada or whoever was with us would urge us to come along. Probably every god in whom any villager was interested was represented. Mother said there were both Buddhist and Taoist dieties there.

Across the street and stretching almost to the end of the village was a big truck garden. A low wall of tamped mud separated the street from the garden. John and I would loiter as long as we could beside that wall for we liked to watch Big Breast Liu, the laborer, irrigate the garden. In summers his back would be burnt to a deep purple, the color of the *kao-liang* bread he ate, and even his heavy breasts would turn bronze color for he worked in his trousers only. He would wind the water up from the well on a tripod windlass, turning it into the little irrigation trenches. He would break the mud walls of the trenches with his bare feet and build them up again in another place, guiding the water. In the autumn he could be seen tying up the big white lettuce-cabbages and carrying them to the "cave," the pit dug in the garden, to keep them from freezing and spoiling through the winter. A low slanting roof covered the pit, one half a roof.

Old Liu, Big Breasted Liu, lived in a little mud brick house in the northwest corner of the garden. A low mud wall fenced it and his little courtyard from the main part of the garden. Usually he lived alone. One year he had a wife. He bought her from the gaunt famine refugees who had come from the western part of the province where, every few years, the Yellow River turned thousands and thousands out of their homes.

To cope with "China's Sorrow," this disastrous natural phenomenon that drowned its thousands, starved its hundreds of thousands, wrecked their homes, and devastated their lands, seemed to me as a child the most important thing to be done, the most wonderful thing that could be done. Something deep within me was hurt each time I heard the river was again on the rampage. Every few years the refugees came, pushing on wheelbarrows their few household goods, and the littlest children, if they had any left, or old people who had not died on the road. They had sold all they had, or almost all, by the time they reached us in the eastern end of the province. Article by article they sold their scanty goods, then their children, and then their women, that they and the children and women might eat and live. Even in the house of another one was alive. Any life was better than death.

Liu of the Big Breasts had never been able to save the dower price for a village maiden, even the village widows scorned him and his meager earnings. They said he was not bright, but I noticed that men with farm lands who were not bright had wives. He paid all his savings for the refugee woman with the round flat face (flatter than any in our part of Shantung province), with big feet like a man's, the toes barely turned under in a token binding (they must have worked their women in the fields in the western part of the province), who stepped over the low mud wall like a man instead of decorously and helplessly sitting on the top as a woman should, swinging her legs over after her. Later she disappeared. Whether she ran away with another man or had simply rejoined her husband as he returned to the west, to put in a new crop, no one ever knew, or cared.

As we passed the gate of Chang the washman I wished I could see the baby, now quite a little boy, who had been left on his doorstep in a basket. Everybody said the little boy looked like him. I was not surprised that his wife, who had no son, was glad to have this boy. She had four daughters, like steps, as they walked in order of their ages across the Ancestral Hall Courtyard when they came to church service. After all, also, many men had concubines and the children of the concubines belonged to the wife. Whoever had borne this "secret child" was not an acknowledged concubine, and even if she were from a "dark gate," whatever child she bore belonged to the wife of the man, should the wife want the child. I wondered who the woman was. Mother did not know and Dada did not tell us. "Probably from another village," Mother said, "brought here by the midwife who delivered her."

Opposite the garden and stretching even further along the village street were the houses of the poor, their gates unpainted and the plaster on the walls around their courtyards falling off and leaving big patches of brown mud for the rains to enter and bring the walls down at the next rainy season.

Outside our village, as outside every village, was the *t'u-ti-miao*, "the temple of the Earth God," the spirit magistrate of our little piece of earth. The little low temple was three or four hundred yards from the east end of the village. Between three and four feet high, it was of mud brick, white plastered under a grey tiled roof. It stood on a little hill where our village street, turned into a country road, met a minor highway. There was a tiny paved terrace, about six feet square, in front of the temple. An old gnarled tree grew beside it and to the right, as we faced the little house in which the tiny figures of the god and his wife sat in their official robes.

The tree beside the temple became potent one year, filled with power, they said, of some spirit. People came from far and near to take a hundful of its leaves to brew into tea for their illnesses. The ground was covered with the ash of the incense they offered. The fragrance of the incense reached the village when the wind was right. Gradually the tree became covered with yellow banners, pieces of yellow cotton cloth about two feet long and eight inches wide, on which were written, horizontally, in black

ink, the four large characters, *ch'ing yeh pi ying*, "Ask and
Ye Shall Receive." I puzzled over this use of the same
words as in the Bible, when the people did not know the
Bible and were praying to "heathen gods."

How did they know the tree was potent? How did
they know that a healing spirit was for a time making it
a resting place? Perhaps someone passing by had looked
up at the grand old tree and his heart had lifted, and he
had gone home to get well. Perhaps someone took a nap
on the terrace beneath the tree and dreamed a dream.
Perhaps someone thought it was time to make a little
money and started the rumor. To sell incense in off
seasons between festivals is not easy.

The *T'u-ti*, the "Earth God" or ruler, the god of the
village, was a very lowly deity. In the pantheon of Heaven
he is the smallest of all officials, but he was a very important god. He kept the census of the village. To him
was announced every death as soon as the breath had left
the body. The heir of the dead man or woman, or a
relative, took the staff and someone took the bowl of
gruel. Three times toward Heaven was the staff pointed
and three times it was pounded on the terrace, calling
Heaven and Earth to witness the announcement. The
bowl of gruel was poured on the bricks in front of the
temple. The little *T'u-ti* was then to carry the news of
the death to the great officials in whose account books all
human deeds, good and bad, were recorded. This was to
set in motion all the things that must be done to the soul
in the great journey through the courts of justice, through
the series of punishments and rewards, which would go on
until the soul was reborn and again started another earthly
journey.

14

THE LONG HAIRED ONES

THE FIRST JOURNEY OUTSIDE our home that I remember was into the southern hills, to Shang-chuang, the High Town, where the people lived in a sunny valley by burning limestone into lime. The church in this small town had invited the yearly association of all the Baptist churches of East Shantung Province to meet with their church. Father and Mother had decided to go and take all of us children. Great excitement for John and me. This town was one the T'ai-p'ings, the Long Haired Ones, those whom some people called the T'ai-p'ing rebels, had raided.

We were brought up on tales of the Long Haired Ones. They were as common in the speech and thought of the time as the stenciled pattern was to the cloth so many of us wore, and as were the pockmarks on the faces of so large a proportion of the men and women. Those times were fresh in the minds of all the people. There were those around us who had been young men and women when the troubles of the T'ai-p'ing years had reached them and were now in their deep middle years, and those who had been children were now mature. There was not a man or a woman over forty who had not personal memories of that time of horror. There was not a person in the countryside whose "heart did not hang loose" when he heard the tales told night after night (as families sat on their *k'ang* in the long winter evenings or squatted on the threshing floors in the long summer twilight guarding their grain) and heard of the slaughter, of those who had died, in those troubled years.

The *T'ai-p'ing t'ien-kuo*, the "Great Peaceful Heavenly Kingdom," had tried (from 1850 to 1864) to take the throne away from the decadent Manchu Dynasty, whose time had come to pass into history. The Heavenly Emperor had set up his throne in Nanking and ruled a large section the land. In 1853 and 1854 his armies had marched northward toward Peking, the seat of the Manchu government. They got as far as the western part of Shantung Province and on to Tientsin before they were turned back by the imperial troops. They never came to the eastern part of the province where we lived, to the cities of Huang-hsien, P'eng-lai and Chefoo, but the bandits of the western part of the province, always abundant in number, due, to a great extent, to the often recurrent overflow of the Yellow River, had seized this opportunity of the northward march of the T'ai-p'ing Army to call themselves T'ai-p'ings. Some of those marauding across Shantung Province might even have been part of the Nien, another organized rebellion of peasants (1851-1868) and located in the northern provinces. These bands, bandits, Nien, and even perhaps

stray lots of T'ai-p'ings drove eastward to the rich part of
the province, looting, killing, raping, and burning as they
went.

These bandits, whether T'ai-p'ings, or Nien, or
independent dispossessed, were called the Long Haired
Ones, the *ch'ang mao-tzu*, because as a sign of rebellion
they refused to shave their hair an inch back of the hair
line as had been decreed by their Manchu rulers, and to
braid their long hair into queues. They combed their long
hair upward, bound it at the crown with cord, and looped
it into coils on top of their heads in the Ming Dynasty
style. In battle these coils would come loose and the long
hair would flow behind them, like black banners, out from
the top of their heads.

There were two walls around our city two *li* (two
thirds of a mile) away, the solid crenelated wall of dressed
stone, like huge bricks, and the outer wall of tamped earth
covered with a thick layer of mixed lime and sand that had
grown hard and grey and lichen-covered with the years
until it also seemed made of stone. This outer wall, this
Wall of Protection, had been built by the people of the
villages and markets clustering around the city gates to
guard against the Long Haired Ones. Most of the larger
villages throughout the plain and in the lower hills had
crumbling earthen walls around them that had been put
up at that time.

Perhaps there were real patriots among those who
marched eastward, who hoped to help free the people
from debt and make the distribution of land the rebel
dynasty called for, but perhaps all such men were with the
real T'ai-p'ing Army. The tales we heard were all of
slaughter and destruction. Those who had had personal

experience with the Long Haired Ones were romantic figures to John and me.

Sa Shih-fu, the Master Workmen Sa, our carpenter, was a silent man. He was not like the cook, always chattering, but sometimes he could be induced to say something. I liked to go into the reception room on the Entrance Court which had been turned into a carpenter's shop. There Sa made copies from pictures of Grand Rapids furniture. I did not like the furniture; it was dull and had no dignity. I would not look at it, but I liked the feel of the sawdust under my feet and I liked the smell of the wood. Sa Shih-fu had been a boy of eight or nine when the Long Haired Ones had come through our part of the country.

"Sa Shih-fu, what did the Long Hairs do in your village?"

"Killed all the old men and old women and the babies."

"Why didn't you all run away?"

"Didn't have time."

"Why didn't you have time?"

"Thought our village was safe. High in the hills. It was a small group of Long Hairs that came to our village." He sighed. "But our village was a small village."

"Why weren't you killed?"

"I was a strong little boy. They liked to have strong little boys to bring up in their camps. They kept the strong young men to work for them and the young women for concubines."

"What work did they make you do?"

"I helped to look after the horses of the chief. He saw that I got enough to eat and that they did not beat

me. I was his favorite." Sa Shih-fu would never elaborate
on that.

There was a farmer who came to church sometimes
in winter when there was no work on the land. (In summer Father and Mr. Chu would visit the villages to keep in
touch with the church members without their having to
come to church, so the farmers would not lose precious
farming days.) This man was tall and broad and made
broader still by the thick cotton-padded coat and trousers
he wore. He dressed differently from our villagers, who
were artisans and tradesmen working in the city or farmers
beginning to dress like city people. He wore the clothes of
the countryside when he was young. His long white cotton-padded socks were pulled up over his trousers and
came almost to his knees. The people around us wore their
trousers over their socks and bound them in at the ankle.
He was the only one who wore the old-fashioned shoes
turned up in front like the prows of little Chinese boats.
The people around us wore shoes with a seam from the
middle toe to the instep, finished off with a ridge of bright
green leather. He wore the old-fashioned hat of black felt,
like the pork pie hat of Western countries only more
flattened. The "modern" Chinese of the time wore little
melon-section skull caps with the red button on top
and, if the weather were cold, padded flannel or satin
wind-hoods over them. His coat was wide and came
almost to his knees (new styles called for coats nearing the
ankle in length) and was bound in with a girdle.

From his girdle, on the left side, hung his long blackwood tobacco pipe with the white soapstone mouthpiece
and the tiny brass bowl which held a wad of tobacco no
larger than an outsized pea; the pouch for his tobacco,

made of blue cotton cloth and decorated with green leather appliqué; and the little leather wallet with the thick iron blade. In the wallet he kept flint and tinder. Matches were new and expensive and not easy for a farmer to get. Most of them carried these "fire wallets." It fascinated me to watch these farmers fill their pipes, lay a tiny bit of tinder on top of the tobacco already packed in the bowl of the pipe, then strike flints with the thick iron blade until the sparks flew. There was skill needed and pride in skill was shown. I would stand, a tiny figure, and look up at those sturdy men, look at them with admiration as they talked slowly to each other, smiled slowly, filled their pipes and smoked. I did not know why I admired them but now, as I look back, I see them confident in their ability to do what needed to be done, full of self respect and respect for others, and dignity.

This farmer, with his old-fashioned clothes, had a broad flat face and a pleasant smile. He found life good, but it had not started that way. When he was a child, three or four years old, the Long Haired Ones had burned his village and slaughtered all who had not had time to run to the hills. Days later, when those who had been in the hills returned, they found him playing among the charred ruins. The only other living thing in the village was the hen whose daily egg he had been searching for when the bandits came. He had crawled, following the hen, into the fire hole of the k'ang, the mud brick bed of North China. He had kept quiet and remained cowering when he heard the commotion outside.

These mud brick flues of the k'ang saved the little boy from the fires which burned the beams and the rafters, the doors and the windows, and from the falling tiles and

the walls of mud brick. Every day the hen laid an egg and
every day he had eaten it.

We travelled to Shang-chuang in a mule litter. The
mules had a difficult time climbing the stone-paved
mountain roads, bound together as they were by the litter
they were carrying between them, lashed on stiff poles,
and the stones polished to glasslike slipperiness by the
constant travel of many feet. The unpaved roads were also
difficult as they twisted and wound up the mountain
valleys.

"Mother, I want to get out and walk. I want to walk
up those steps."

"Those are not steps. They are terraces; each step,
as you call it, is several feet high. You could scarcely
climb them even." So the hills receded and took on
dimension, and the stairway to Heaven became the terraced
fields going up the mountain side, with rough stone retaining walls grown black with age. (Our own country was
flat with the rich fields spreading wide from village to vil-
liage, each a few *li* from the next.)

Nestled in a crotch of the hills, opening south to
the sun and sheltered from the north winds of winter, was
Shang-chuang, "the Upper Village." The houses were built
of field stone set in lime plaster. There was plenty of lime
in the hills. On the shoulders of several hills could be
seen the slow smoke curling upward from the mud domes
under which stones were being burnt into lime. In another
valley was another village, one with enough converts to
have its own chapel: Hui-ch'eng Ch'i chia, the Ch'i Family
Village with a Wall of Lime.

The women of Upper Village gave me a doll made of
white cotton cloth stuffed with cotton wool. In the

sewed-together hands of the doll was a brightly colored
peach: one of the most common symbols of longevity and
fertility. Down the back was the strip of red cloth that
was down the back of the coats of every baby for its
first few months. This strip of red cloth, guarding the
spine and the unshaved spot on top of the baby's head
guarding the fontanelle, were to keep in the soul, to keep
the spirit from leaving the body through the seams not
yet firmly knit. Under the apron, like the red apron worn
by all the little boys, was what all little boys had,
beautifully stitched and shaped. They called it a birdie.
Mother told them to rip it off before she let me have the
doll. I could not understand why. All little boys had
them. I saw the little boys all summer running around in
their little red aprons or with nothing on at all. At any
time, even in the winter, a little boy wearing the split
trousers of childhood might squat and show that he was
a boy. Why should not a doll have one too? Was mother
changing the doll to a girl doll? No. A girl had something
too, only different. Of course a Chinese doll would be
a boy doll, for boys were more important than girls. But
now the doll was nothing. I was never very fond of that
mutilated doll. Nor could the Chinese women understand.
Another of the incomprehensible ways of the people from
across the ocean: to deny so simple and obvious a thing.

One of the little boys I played with lived near where
we were staying and belonged to the same family. His
grown-up wife helped our hostess. He had been left an
orphan when very young. His relatives had, therefore,
married him to a grown girl of eighteen for someone to
take care of him and of his property.

The people of Upper Village had thought they were
too far up in the hills for the bandits to trouble them and
so had not had time, when they heard the Long Haired
Ones were coming, to take the women and children to
the hills higher up: the women who could not go fast
because of their little bound feet.

The soil around the mountain village was poor.
Sweet potatoes—poor man's food, was their chief crop.
They ate the potatoes boiled; they ate them roasted. They
cut the potatoes in slices and dried them. They pounded
the dried potato into powder and, mixing it with their
wheat flour, made bread. They had deep pits where they
put the potatoes in winter to keep them from freezing.

When the people in the village heard the Long Haired
Ones were coming they lowered the women into these
pits, the women and the little children. They put poles
across the pits and spread matting across the poles. They
covered the matting with newly harvested beans to dry.
They were careful to leave the main supply of beans where
the bandits could get it easily and not bother to disturb
that which was drying.

The men then fled into the hills.

The women of the village looked kind to me, even
the older ones. Perhaps the ones who had had to do the
deed I had been told about were now dead. I looked at
all the grandmothers, the ones who were grandmothers
now, and wondered if any of them had used their hands
in ways so terrible. They were the ones who had been
young mothers when the Long Haired Ones had come
across the country.

Down in the pit, that day, the little children crouched
with their mothers, silent with fear. A Chinese child

learns early to know the attitudes of the grown people always around him. They heard the bandits come. They heard their shouts as they found and seized the foodstuffs they were after.

The mothers pressed their babies against their breasts. "Eat and sleep," they prayed. One whisper would betray them all to the bandits and all would be killed and those not killed dragged off to serve their captors. The mothers' hands stayed near the throats of their babies. Any cry must be stifled. They knew it was better to lose one life than to lose all their lives and everyone was responsible for all.

When the men returned they found their women and children safe. But at least one or two of the women held dead babies in their arms.

15

WE RANGE FURTHER ABROAD

As WE GREW OLDER we ranged, John and I, farther and farther into the countryside, taking walks often by ourselves, sometimes with the parents, and sometimes with the young cook who had taken Chiang Wen-chi's place when he set up as a farmer.

A walk with a destination is the best kind of walk provided one is not rigid about how to get there: the best features of both the walk with a destination and the roaming walk are therefore combined. Our most common destination was Hsiao Lan Chia T'an, the Smaller Lan Family Village, where the other missionaries who had joined my parents now lived.

The shortest way to get there was by the path along the foot of the Wall of Protection, between the wall and the dry moat, planted to wheat and lined with poplar trees. In autumn the little boys of the nearby villages, the little girls whose feet were not yet being bound, and the

171

old women, came to gather what they could find to burn.
The children made a game of collecting the big poplar
leaves. They strung them on strings—the big beautiful
green and gold leaves, and compared the length of their
strings and the sizes of the leaves they had collected.
Sometimes the little boys would stop to chase a late
autumn butterfly.

Sometimes by the side of the path under the Wall of
Protection or lying against one of the low grave mounds
would be what looked like a bundle of millet stalks, such
as were piled in a corner of an inn courtyard or a farmyard,
waiting to be cut up and fed to the mules and donkeys.
But we knew no farmer would throw away such a bundle,
allow such waste. We knew there was wrapped in that
straw a newborn baby who had died, or a small baby too
young for a coffin. They were thrown in this way to the
dogs, since it was believed these babies' lives had been
taken by evil spirits jealous of human life, especially the
life of boys, and that these evil spirits often inhabited the
bodies of dogs. If the tiny dead body was thrown to
the dogs, perhaps the spirits would let the next child live.

Sometimes we would see a new grave, a long low
heap of earth only, no great round mounds, for this was
public land where only the very poor and the paupers were
buried. The graves were so shallow that sometimes the
dogs, the hungry, homeless dogs, and sometimes those
that were not homeless but were nevertheless hungry, dug
down to the thin boards of the cheap coffins. When that
happened, so that we should not see the torn bodies, we
were taken to Hsiao Lan Chia T'an through the Wall of
Protection, across the city parade ground, near where

Dr. Fan lived, and through the shop-lined street just inside the East Gate.

Sometimes we would walk along the Sha Ho, the Sand River, that width of yellow sand, bordered on either side by a row of willow trees. For most of the year the river wound through this expanse of sand, a thin stream, crossed by an outsized wooden bench. Only during the summer rains would the water, a thick muddy flood, reach from bank to bank, and carry away more of the farmers' precious land.

The Wang Family Village where lived Dog's Mother and the five brothers all named Dog, First Dog, Second Dog, and so on, was beside this river. The five boys were all called Dog, hoping the evil spirits would be loath to take the lives of those bearing the names of their allies.

Mrs. Wang, the mother of the five Dog brothers, was a striking figure. When I first became conscious of her, she was dressed all in white, in mourning for her husband. She gave him the full twenty-seven months of mourning, as the first of the pair to die and therefore take precedence and be mourned as a parent is mourned. Eventually she laid aside her mourning, but to me she will always be a figure dressed in white, with long foot-wide sleeves and a wide white coat to her knees, her white trousers bound tightly at her ankles. Her feet were very small. The bound-foot mince superimposed on her naturally masterful stride made her look, as she walked on the narrow raised footpaths between the fields, like a great white heron flapping its wings and strutting as it flapped, or like a ship in full sail in a gale. I would watch her on the rare occasions when she came to church and wonder about the secret little smile that did not involve her eyes. They

were always hidden, remote. The four older Dogs farmed
her land. The land was family land but we always thought
of it as her land. Fifth Dog came to Mother's school. The
others were already too old when the school started. They
all had school names, however, dignified school names,
but we knew them by their milk-names, as the five Dogs.

The wind blew the stories about Mrs. Wang, Dogs'
Mother, and from the little breezes dropped words.

"She is too *li-hai*—she is cruel!"

"Another daughter-in-law has run away, has returned
to her own mother."

"She is too *li-hai*—she destroys."

"Her sons sleep on her *k'ang* even after they are
married."

"She is too *li-hai*—she takes all the good and leaves to
others only that which injures."

"She works her daughters-in-law too hard."

"She is too *li-hai.*"

The stories about Mrs. Wang blew with the wind and
from the little breezes dropped words.

One day as we walked home from Hsiao Lan Chia
T'an we saw the woman who lived in the little house by
the side of the road as it dipped to the river crossing. It
was a little one-room house made of kao-liang stalks
covered over with mud. It was not large enough for a
family. There was no wall around it, no courtyard, but
a kao-liang stalk and mud fence shielded the entrance and
curved around to the side. The fence was higher than a
man is tall.

"Who lives there?" I asked. "It looks lonely and
too small for a family." Also it was too well kept for
beggars.

"A woman."

"A woman all alone?"

"Yes, a woman all alone."

"Why does she live there all alone? Hasn't she any family? How does she get money to live?"

"Men come to see her."

This was no answer, as far as I could see, but I also could see that I would get no more.

We saw her that day. She was a drab-looking woman and I wondered what men saw in her. She was over thirty, I should say, and looked like an ordinary housewife of the more self-indulgent type, and as if she took opium. It was just a job to be done, a way to earn her living, and perhaps that of others besides, in the little house on the side of the highway where men came and went.

There were no bad droughts to destroy the crops in our narrow coastal plain. The floods sometimes washed away bridges and peddlers' stalls by the city gate but did not do too much damage to the fields. But we had locusts, occasionally, and one year we had caterpillars.

We heard there were caterpillars in the village to the north and west. It was late afternoon. The sun was setting as we walked toward it across the fields on our way home. There was a golden light in the sky and across the dark green of the field of beans in front of us, and another field beyond that did not look as rich.

A man was walking toward us on the path beaten hard by the pat of many cloth-soled shoes. He stepped aside and squatted between the rows of beans. We came nearer. From his clothes he would seem to be a prosperous farmer on his way home from a visit to relatives or on his way to a meeting with the village headmen. He was obviously in his best clothes. They were clean and the creases were still in his white cotton coat and black cotton trousers where they had been folded and laid away in the box, made as all clothes should be made, to fold and be laid away flat. His hat—a great circle of straw—was of the better and more durable kind and the strings were carefully sewn ribbons of blue cloth, the same as that which lined the brim. His shoes were the better shoes of a farmer, stout black cloth.

His face was tense as he lifted a branch of a bean plant and saw what he saw. There was no bitterness. There was no despair. There was an evaluation of the situation, as he looked at the beans and at the ground, that took count of what this destruction of the crop meant to all. I saw the recognition of hunger and want in his face, the recognition of inevitable suffering. He dropped his hand with a gesture of finality, stood up, and walked away.

In front of us as far as we could see was a field of bare bean stalks, without a leaf, without a pod, standing straight and low. Over our feet, around us, over and under the bean plants flowed a carpet of black caterpillars. We turned. The rich green field through which we had just passed was now a thicket of bare stalks.

More suffering for the people, not as many people as that heart-breaking time when the Yellow River broke its dikes, but as desperate for those whose fields were desolated. What could anyone do?

We did not often go beyond our village or the fields around it, except to Hsiao Lan Chia T'an where lived the Stephens family, but sometimes the young man who was cook after Chiang Wen-chi became a farmer would take

us with him to the market which came every three days.
It was fun to go into the city, through the Great City
Gates and on the city streets, but we could not see much
where people crowded. We had grown beyond the stage
of seeing only blue clad legs moving scissorlike, but the
blue clad bodies were equally effective in coming between
us and what there was to see.

In the grain shops, where we went to get the money,
we would see great square bins, with half-open faces, in
a row across the shop, filled with the little brownish grey
wheat grains, with the tiny golden millet grains, the
greenish yellow soybeans, the golden brown and purple
kao-liang, larger than wheat. In a small bin to one side
would be the white, white rice that the southerners liked
so much and only the rich in Huang-hsien bought. The
cook would take us to the meat selling shops and to the
stalls where vegetables were bought, though these he got
mostly from our own village.

As we went to the market section, inside the West
Gate of the Wall of Protection, we passed through the
back streets where the "little inns" were located and
smelled the sweet sickening smell of opium coming over
the walls. "Bad," said the young cook.

The young cook took us to an inn yard to see our
first camels. They lay, great heaps of dirty brown wool,
on the ground with their snakelike necks lowered and
their dragon heads busy chewing their cuds. They were
resting, for in our part of the country they had to travel
by night as they frightened the mules and donkeys who
had never before seen such grotesque creatures. They did
not come often enough to make it worth the time of the

local farmers to accustom their animals to the sight and smell of them.

The young cook took us to temple fairs, and bought us glazed red-fruit, eight to a stick, with hearts of ground sesame seeds and chips of green plums; balls of sticky malt candy, the kind used to sweeten the kitchen god's mouth at New Year time so he would report only good of the family when he had been sent by fire to the courts above; and the little red blown-glass toys, like tiny trumpets with a tympanum of glass. They usually shattered with the third outward blow or inward suck of the breath.

Pu tung, pu tung pah	*Pu tung, pu tung*—the sound as the glass tympanum blew in and out,
Pu tung, pu tung	and *pah*, the sound as the glass broke.)
Tao pu liao chia	Home cannot be reached (before the toy broke).

To avoid this calamity I usually refused to blow mine until we got back home, but even then I did not always arrive with the frail toy intact. We saw the little paper whirligigs, with tiny paper banners of many colors flying in the wind or turned by the hands of those who gambled for a few pieces of candy.

The young cook would not allow us to look into the peep shows until he had looked first and after much pleading from us. The men seemed to have such a good time with their eyes against the little glass slots, but the general we saw strutting across the stage, when at last we were allowed to look, was not very interesting. I had

seen the cook speaking to the man who ran the show.
After all we had not been allowed, it would seem, to see
what others saw. Years later, when I saw Chinese por-
nographic pictures, I could imagine what the cook had not
allowed us to see.

Buying Christmas presents was always a problem.
The Montgomery Ward boxes had to come in the summer
because the little coastal trade junks did not sail in the
winter storms and our little harbor was inadequate for
refuge. It was not in human nature to keep anything
hidden so many months from each other. Since Chinese
New Year came after Christmas we could not count on
the toys that came on the market at that time. There
was not much to buy in the ordinary shops that would
have made a child's Christmas, at least so thought our
young cook.

He took John and me to the best store in town and
helped us pick our presents to each other. It was the only
store that had imported goods—imported from Japan. We
sat in solemn dignity in the inner office of the shop,
beside the big square table, drinking tea, while the cook
and the clerk talked their desultory polite talk. Then John
went into the outer shop while I chose a gift for him as
the clerk set out his wares on the table, one by slow one.
Then I went into the outer room while John chose a gift
for me. I worried, fearing we might buy the same thing
for each other, but I underestimated our young cook.
There was a glass globe I bought for John: when shaken,
little golden flakes floated. There was a kaleidoscope
through which I never tired of looking, with its endless
variety of formal patterns, which I hoped John would give
me.

We never saw any policeman. No one controlled the traffic. The rules of the road were known to all. Sometimes there was a jam with much shouting which all the by-standers enjoyed.

As we grew older, John and I would sometimes walk out alone, with only each other. "Which is which? Evidently they are a boy and a girl—they are dressed differently, but which is the boy and which is the girl?" we heard one countryman say to another as we walked by.

One day we walked through the back street of a village not far from home. A woman sat on a bench outside her gate. We seldom stopped to talk with the villagers unless they asked us to, but she looked so unhappy, and she raised her head as we came by and we saw her sad eyes. We gave her the usual greeting, "Is all well with you?"

She looked even more unhappy. "No, I am sick. I will soon be dead. The sooner the better."

My heart was touched and, patterned after Mother's best manner, I said to her, "You must not be unhappy, there's a Heaven to go to and God is. . . ."

"Why have another world? There's enough trouble in this one. When I reincarnate I want to come back as an animal—a donkey or a pig. It is too difficult to be a human being."

We went on a picnic to the sand dunes by the sea, eighteen *li* (six miles) away. We children, the lunch, and the "boy" went in a farm cart drawn by two grey mules, one hitched in front of the other. The wheels made a pleasant grinding, sliding sound as they went through the sand. Mother and the other women went in sedan chairs, carried by three men each, one to spell off the others.

Father and the other men rode on bicycles.

The drift of sand dunes beside the sea, part of the Gulf of Peichihli, was high, the sand held by coarse grass and stunted pine trees. On the lee side were cemeteries, burial places of families thrifty enough to spare their fields and rich enough to own the dunes and to keep the graves in shape. We chose the graveyard of some notable family for our picnic. This was common Chinese practice and no desecration. The grave plots were the only places where trees grew in the open. Graves were placed, if possible, with a hill behind and water running in front, to have the correct Wind and Water influences. People thought of their ancestors as like themselves, except that they lived in another element and could not ordinarily be seen. They had, however, the same tastes and desires.

The low stone table, in front of the high round mound of the main grave, on which the living placed the food for the dead at stated intervals, was big enough to take easily our picnic lunch as we gathered around. The lesser graves, smaller round mounds, straggled up the dune on either side. There was harmony and rhythm in the way they were placed. That, I could feel, but I did not then know about asymmetrical balance or that the placing of graves as well as the building of houses was an art carefully worked out on scientific principles. I knew nothing about geomancy, knew no master of Wind and Water, a man who spent his life studying these matters from ancient books.

The sun shone on the grasses and on the sand, shades of yellow punctuated with accents of green. The world was a beautiful place. Cemeteries were not gloomy places. Why did some of the grownups talk about lying in the grave a thousand years, until the Judgment Day? Even the golden streets of Heaven seemed unpleasant to me, hard and glaring, and I knew I would be bored twanging a harp all the time. To pass through the eighteen hells and judgments and be reborn, though rugged, was a much more pleasant prospect. Active and alive. I ran away from the solemn talk. I saw John down in the little harbor, the mouth of the Sandy River, clambering over the fishing boats and talking to the fishermen. I ran down and joined him.

16

INTO THE HILLS

Our SECOND NOTABLE EXCURSION outside our compound, our village, and our hsien, our county, was to Pei-kou, "the North Gully." Strictly speaking it was not within the radius of our lives in Sung-chia-t'an. It was in the P'eng-lai district and not in Huang-hsien, but our hostess, Wang Lao T'ai-t'ai, "the Honorable Madame Wang," was one of Mother's friends. Sometimes she came to visit us, riding on a big black mule, for the roads were rough over the ragged hills, and now we were going to visit her.

Lao T'ai-t'ai was one of those legendary figures that got mixed up for me with the shadowy emperor in Peking, and God and Grandmother Seward, and Queen Victoria. She was the only woman in the church connection who was ever called Lao T'ai-t'ai, literally "the Great Exalted," the term used for the wives of officials. Other women were addressed by an honorary family title such as Honor-

able Aunt, or Elder Sister-in-law, according to their age
in relation to the age of the one addressing them, or more
familiarly as the Mother of whatsoever was the name of
her eldest child. But Wang Lao T'ai-t'ai was easier to sort
out and get fixed in time and space than the Emperor in
Peking and Grandma Seward in Ohio.

She was called Lao T'ai-t'ai not because she was old,
though she seemed old enough to John and me. She must
have been in her middle or late forties when the twins
were married. She was called Lao T'ai-t'ai because she
was the dowager of the not inconsiderable household,
the grandmother of the young lords, and because the land
the family owned and she controlled was great, but
mainly because her husband had been an official, although
a small one.

"They have rooms in their compound piled to the
ceiling with strings of cash."

"She keeps silver ingots buried in her room."

"She has silver in all her boxes."

She had first become interested in the Gospel in the
troubled days after the death of her only son, when the
Gospel and Mrs. Crawford (a missionary in P'eng-lai) had
been her chief comforts. Some hated her enough to say
that "foreign protection," or rather the possibility of
foreign protection, had been what had comforted her.
She and Mrs. Crawford had become "sworn daughter and
mother."

Others had been unkind enough to say that an added
reason and a very important one for her joining the church
had been to avoid the annual village tax to be used for
keeping up the temples and for the observance of the
festivals with theatricals and in other suitable ways.

Although she gave money to the church, she never gave
as much as she would have had to give to the village elders.
"But you must not judge her," Father would say gently,
"it is between God and her conscience."

Her two grandsons attended Mother's school. They
were twins. One of them, the elder, was tall for his age
(the boys were about twelve when they first came to
school), well built and vigorous. He had the high cheek-
bones, the strong jaw, and the brown skin of the Shantung peasant, and a length of face that made credible his
birth into a gentry family. The other boy was small for
his age and small of bone. He was delicate and his skin
was pale olive. He would have been good looking in a
highbred way if he had not had a harelip. Nor was it an
ordinary harelip. The jaw was split also, and the front
teeth and their gum pushed through the slit in the left
side of his upper lip. He was the better student, though
the other did not lack brains.

They were both engaged to be married even before
they came to school, had been engaged since they were
babies. Such an important matter in such an important
family could not have been left too long after they were
born. Now they were to be married. They were fifteen
by Chinese count. Perhaps they had passed their four-
teenth birthday. It was to be a double wedding.

Just before the wedding, however, the girl to whom
the older twin was engaged died. The preparations for
the younger twin's wedding went on as planned. The next
generation must be assured as soon as possible.

We were invited to the wedding. We were to be there
several days before the great event. Pei-kou was thirty *li*
from Hang-hsien, where the hills that formed the eastern

end of the province began to give way to good farm land. When the boys came to school they usually rode on donkeys; the road was too rough, as a usual thing, for carts. But since the wedding was in the summer and the rains had not yet broken, the roads were still in fair condition. We were to go by cart.

It was exciting that we were to go by sedan cart. It was exciting to have them send their cart for us. But the stiff heavy wooden frame bumped one's head as it jolted over the ruts in the road, if one was not careful, and I was always afraid it would overturn. We heard dreadful stories of broken legs and the bones sticking out. But worst of all it was even more difficult to see out of a cart than out of a *shen-tzu*, the mule litter, especially if John were along, for as a boy he sat in front and blocked my view. I would really rather have ridden in a basket on one side of a mule with John in the basket on the other, as we sometimes did when we went to P'eng-lai, while, sometimes, Dada sat in the middle on the saddle, even though it was somewhat frightening to swing through the air. We could then see everything there was to see. Best of all would have been to ride in a chair. But they were sending the cart to fetch us.

Pei-kou sat on the top of two hills with a deep gully through which the road wound up. A compound surrounded by a newly white plastered wall—this always attracted attention and usually meant a wedding or a funeral—was at the top of one hill. The ridge poles and tiled roofs of a landlord showed over the walls. Some other houses in the village had tiled roofs, but most of them were thatched. We were driven to the threshing floor in the back of the compound and taken to the guest court and the house of the guest court.

John and I spent most of our time running back and forth through the gate between the guest court and the main compound, trying to keep up with all that was going on while Father and Mother talked with the other wedding guests. Sometimes we peeked into Lao T'ai-t'ai's room where she and Mother and the other women sat on the k'ang and talked—the k'ang with the kao-liang straw matting mellowed to a deep burnt amber that reflected the sunlight as it poured softly through the white paper windows, lit the wine red chests against the wall, and melted into the indigo blue of the quilts piled on one end of the k'ang. We tried to peek into the inner room to see the strings of cash but the door was shut. We never found out if the stories of the hoarded wealth were true.

To be able to cook the food needed for the feasting, a temporary kitchen had been set up. Straw mats roofed over one corner of the main courtyard, the Women's Court. Stoves of mud brick had been built with the great castiron cooking basins mortared into place. Boards on saw-horses for tables and chopping blocks were set up. Itinerant cooks who went from wedding to wedding or funeral took charge. John and I spent much of our time watching them.

The day before the wedding was hectic. The cooks made bread. They kneaded the great piles of risen dough into round loaves and steamed them. Their rich fragrance, the rich nutty fragrance of freshly ground flour in which all the values were still left, permeated the compound. That night they pulled the dough as candy is pulled at a village fair in America. They called it "throwing the noodles" or "thrown noodles." A strong man pulled the dough out into as long a shape as he could and then slammed it onto the kneading board covered with flour, doubled the dough over on iself, pulled again, and again slammed it onto the kneading board. This went on until the dough was in strings no thicker than twine, like spaghetti. Great strength and dexterity were needed to make "thrown noodles" and they were considered a special treat and better than the usual chopped noodles. We stood and watched and watched, nor did the cook who made thrown noodles, and thrown noodles only, allow his moment in the public eye to lack drama. High above his head he held the great mass of dough ready to slam it onto the board. He heaved his chest as he pulled the dough out, spreading his arms wide, and raised it again above his head. The slam on the kneeding board came from a taut body bent like a bow. At no time did his arms work alone. As in almost all activity the whole of the man was involved and it became a kind of dance. Since he was stripped to the waist the full play of his smooth muscles could be seen and the firelight gleaming on his brown skin shining with sweat.

The thrown noodles, however, seemed hard and tasteless to me when at last I had some to eat and not as good as the chopped noodles. When I tried beaten biscuits, that vaunted Southern delicacy in the United States, I began to understand that the extra value of these two gourmet specialties came from the labor it took to make them. The hostess had the satisfaction of knowing that her guests knew that she had money enough to command the needed skill and labor and had spent it on them, and the guests were pleased to be the recipients of that money, time, and labor.

There was chopping, chopping, chopping, as the meats and vegetables were prepared—chopped on the wooden blocks, cross sections of trees, that are in every North China kitchen. Nothing came to the table in any piece that could not be picked up by a pair of chopsticks and put into the mouth. Many of the dishes required the meats to be as finely chopped and mixed as though they had been through a grinder. The chopping was like the chopping one hears on nights before the New Year in all the villages and cities, the sound of which to any Chinese away from home is one of the most poignant.

All through the compound crept rich fragrances of cooking meats and spices—anise and *hua-chao*, green peppers, garlic, ginger, and soya sauce, especially just after a new batch of meat and vegetables had been thrown into the hot fat, after the splash and sizzle, when the rich smells rose with the hot steam.

The great day arrived. The groom had been gone for hours when we awoke, gone in the green chair to fetch the bride. A young cousin, a boy of ten, had sat in the red chair when they went to fetch the bride. He was the *ya-chiao-ti*, the one who "weighted the chair" until the bride should sit in it.

They came in through the front gate. I surged along with the crowd as the bride's matrons drew her forward, the tall red-swathed figure following the little half-grown boy who was becoming her husband, for the bride was eighteen years old. It was necessary that she be strong enough to bear the needed children soon and also that she be strong enough to do her share of the work in the family. In farming districts it was customary for the wife

to be two or three years or even six years older than her
husband.

Across the front court they went, through the common room of the house where Lao T'ai-t'ai lived in the
two rooms to the east and the mother of the twins in the
two rooms to the west, across the second court to the
threshold of the common room of the house where the
twins were to live with their wives. The room prepared
for the bride was to the east which had precedence over
the room to the west. Though the bridegroom was the
younger twin he was marrying first and so had precedence.

The bride carried a bottle wrapped in red cloth,
carrying it like a baby in the fold of her arm. The word
for bottle is *p'ing* and the word for peace is *p'ing*. The
ideographs are different but the sound is the same. On the
threshold of the house where she was to live, the threshold
she had to cross, was a red saddle, over which she must
step. The word for saddle is *an* and the word for serenity
is *an*. *P'ing* and *an* together makes *p'ing-an*, the common
word for peace. Spoken Chinese is a disyllabic language.
The family was doing all it could to ensure peace in the
marriage.

The attendants in their formal robes lifted the red
silk curtain hanging at the door of the bride's room. The
bride's women drew her into the rose-colored light that
filled the room, light that came through the red paper on
the latticed windows, light which seemed almost solid
enough to give way as the figures advanced to the red
k'ang, spread with a red rug over matting made from the
fiber of the red *kao-liang* and piled high on either end with
red quilts of silk or cotton, folded neatly. They helped
her up onto the *k'ang* where she was to sit, passive and

still, legs folded, hands in her lap, a folded red figure, upright on a red k'ang, in a cave of redness, waiting for the man to enter.

It did not occur to me to wonder what the bride would think about a husband with a harelip or even whether she knew he had one until she saw him after she had been placed on the k'ang and he had lifted the thick red veil. Girls married the men their families chose for them. The harelip could have been a point in the bargaining, making possible greater demands from her family.

Managing everything, unobtrusive and competent, was the distant cousin, Lao Wang, an old bachelor who had devoted his life to Lao T'ai-t'ai and the family. He was the perfect example of the faithful servant or steward in the old Chinese feudal pattern—the faithful servant immortalized in Chinese drama, fiction, and history.

I later learned that even he had a story. His mother had bought a little girl to help with the housework and eventually to marry her son. The girl had, one day, displeased the old woman who had then started to beat her. The boy tried to stop his mother. In anger at his unfilial attitude in taking the girl's part, in fear for what the future might bring of more unfilial partiality, she sold the girl to another family. Years later, after half a lifetime of service to Lao T'ai-t'ai, Lao Wang saw this girl again at a temple fair: a fine upstanding matron with her husband and brood of children around her. "Mother, oh Mother," had been wrung from him, "how you have wronged me."

Bit by bit through the years I built up Wang Lao T'ai-t'ai's story, gathered from a word here and a tale there.

Wang Lao T'ai-t'ai, a poor girl, had been taken when she was sixteen years old to be the concubine of a childless official of advanced years. He had died soon after, leaving her with a boy baby and an estate to manage. Together, the two of them—she the young widow and he the portionless cousin who was not much older than she—had brought up the boy and managed the estate. When the boy was fifteen they had married him to a wife. In the first year of marriage he had died, leaving his young wife a few months pregnant.

Like the hordes of Genghis Khan advancing on a land, the relatives bore down on the estate to break the tenuous hold of the two young widows, one in her early thirties and the other not yet twenty, one a mere concubine holding the land through the son who was now dead, and the other, though a wife in status, holding the land through an unborn child who might never be born and who might if born turn out to be a girl. The relatives decided it would be best if the child were never born.

Sudden noises were set off, such as fire crackers and the furious beating of gongs, under the window of the young widow, in the middle of the night, hoping that the fright would cause her to miscarry. Nor did they neglect other means to get the two widows involved and so lose the land. One cousin ordered his old mother to commit suicide outside the gate of the Wang home. He would then be able to claim that they—the widows—had driven his mother to suicide by some mistreatment and thus, by laying the death on them, claim great sums of money. He gave his mother the poison and told her to take it in the Wang family gateway. The next morning she came home. He had not given her enough. The next night he gave her a

larger portion of poison and sent her back. The next
morning she again came home. This time he had given
her too much and she had vomited it all. He did not try
again. Evidently it was his mother's destiny to live—that
the time for her to die had not yet come. He did not,
however, give up trying to get the Wang family property.

"Those nightmare days passed at last." The younger
widow was brought to bed. "All I saw through the mist of
pain and fear was the little red bundle with the deformed
face. But they told me I had twins."

The older twin seemed very well developed for a newborn babe. He looked strangely like the tall vigorous wife
of a loyal cousin-brother who had been pregnant and
whose baby "had died at birth" and who became the
older little lordling's wet nurse. She had been also one of
the women to help the Young Mistress during her labor.
But the frail younger "twin" was a boy and he survived
so the older "twin's" right to share the property was
never challenged. Their names were entered in the family
records, Wang Fu-chao and Wang Fu-hsi, and no one of
the relatives disputed the older boy's right to have his
name there.

Years later, when I lived in Peking and visited my
old home at intervals, I would ask about the family and
one summer we made a detour from the newly built motor
road to call on them. Wang Lao Tai-t'ai was long since
dead. The frail unobtrusive little woman with the pale
face, whose only meaning in life had been that she was
the mother of twins, was also dead. The house was now
ruled by two more women. One was a vigorous, little,
middle-aged woman who reminded me in some ways of
Lao T'ai-t'ai. I had never before seen this woman. She

had been brought to the home as a bride to the older
twin a year after the wedding we had seen. The other,
tall and colorless, standing around without expression on
her face, had been the bride that day in my childhood.
Both men were out. They were landlords and village
headmen with many duties. The women showed us the
study the younger twin had built on a little rise by the
threshing floor. He kept up the tradition of scholarship and sometimes taught a little village school.

As we went away my friends told me more about
them. The older twin spent freely. That had hurt Lao
T'ai-t'ai. The younger twin had the better head, even for
farming but he was gentle, too gentle. They were good,
however, to the old lady and they had ensured the succession. There were not many great-grandsons but there
were enough. The old lady, the Lao T'ai-t'ai, went to
her grave, however, with her last great wish unfulfilled.
Her eldest grandson, who could have done so had he
wished, had not raised her from the rank of concubine
to that of wife to his grandfather; she had to go through
the next world as she had gone through this, a concubine.

17

FURTHER SHORES

THE TIME HAD COME for us to go to regular schools. We, John and I, had been taking lessons from Father every day, but now we went to the English schools in Chefoo. John went to the Prep School and I entered the lower third form, the lowest in the Girls' School. Besides arithmetic and geography, we had French, Latin, and English history. We seemed always, every term, to start with William the Conqueror and get bogged down in the Wars of the Roses in which all the Plantagenet royalty and nobility killed each other off and gave a new set of people a chance to run the country, while the merchants of London prospered greatly. We also had the Bible as history on weekdays—the epic of David came alive, became whole, a vivid and complicated story—and as religion on Sundays.

We exercised. We played rounders and field hockey. We took long walks. We ranged over the hills, sparsely covered with scrub pine, high above the sea and the islands, old rose in the evening light. The hills curved around East Beach: the crescent of sand and the ring of pink stone houses with red tiled roofs built by the Western merchants, girdled by the highway. Between the beach and the crest were a few sparse acres where farmers scratched out a bare living. We would march up the path beside the pink stone wall that crowned the ridge, built to keep out the Japanese when it was feared they would come overland from Weihaiwei. I was sure this wall looked like the Great Wall of China. Back of the first ridge we could see, when we reached the top, the second ridge crowned with a crumbling wall of blackened stone, built to guard against the T'ai-p'ing armies which, after all, never came this far east. The eastern arm of the curving ridge ended in the Naval Station, high on a bluff above the sea. Sometimes we would see bands of cadets marching into town singing some lusty song from deep in their chests. We were not interested in the cadets nor in the scrub pines the peasants harvested for kindling. We would hunt for the wild carnations that grew among the rocks. The western end of the ridge was a hill that jutted into the sea. The flags of the nations—American, English, Japanese, French, and Russian—flew above their consulates. The mast and yard arms of the signal station crowned the hill. I would watch to see if there were any black balls aloft to tell us a steamer was coming. A double black ball meant a man-of-war. Sitting on the rocks we would watch the steamers from the north, from Tientsin, rounding the big island across the bay, or, if from the south, from Shanghai, steaming along the coast between the little islands and by the lighthouse island. But it was the sea and the pink islands that I looked at most, the sea that never was the same: heavy grey on dull days, as though the

world had melted all its lead and poured it there; blue in
every varying shade as the sunlight glinted; and angry as
the white horses tossed. Even at table I would be looking
at the sea and the pink islands beyond and forget to pass
the bread and butter to my neighbor.

Good also were the friends we made. Sometimes we
would take one or more of them home with us for a
holiday visit. Six times every year we travelled from home
to school or school to home. The seventy miles took us
two days each time, travelling in mule litters. I always
wanted to ride in the litter whose front mule had the red
pompoms on his bridle, but John usually got him, for John
could talk to the muleteers. John knew what the words
meant that the muleteers shouted when they were angry
with the mules, but he would not tell me what they meant.
We would stop for lunch, or rather for the mules to have
lunch, in a village inn, and spend the night in an inn
about halfway. When Mother was with us she would spread
Keatings powder on the *k'ang* and make a little great-wall
of powder around her pallet. The millions of hungry
insects did not seem to bother me, but I liked best to sleep
outdoors in the litter. I liked to go to sleep with the sound
of the mules champing their feed, and sometimes I would
wake in the night to hear the thud of the stick against the
side of the manger as the muleteer mixed the bran with
the fodder for their midnight meal. Sometimes I would
hear the drawn-out crunch as the long heavy blade cut
through the bundles of millet straw to be fed to the
mules. I would wake while it was still dark, when the
light was trying to break into the darkness. I did not have
that gone feeling, that almost sick feeling of waking too
early, if I heard a cock crowing away off to the east,

and then one closer would crow, and then another, even closer, and felt the litter shake as the pig scratched his back on the bamboo slats under me. Gradually the inn yard would appear, developing out of the darkness as one of Mother's photographs developed in the acid bath. Gradually the chill that did not seem to belong to the day that was to come would melt.

While we were at these schools, the Boxer Trouble, as Westerners called the 1900 rebellion, broke over the land: that upsurge of the peasants, another in the long procession of such rebellions that have happened several hundred times in the long history of China. The peasants knew they were hungry. For many, their ways of earning a living had disappeared. Were not those foreign steamships taking the "imperial grain" to Peking instead of the barges on the Grand Canal? How many thousands did not that alone put out of work? Added to the dislocation of the economy caused by the forceable "opening" of China by the West was a severe drought such as periodically troubled the land. The Son of Heaven and his deputies, the Father-Mother magistrates, had very clearly failed in their duty to care for their people. This was the time-honored invitation to rebellion. Surely the Mandate of Heaven had left this dynasty. These same peasants hated the foreign devils, those people from over the ocean, who were corrupting their people, teaching them to change their ways of life, the ways that had served them so many thousands of years. The peasants banded themselves, as they so often did, into a secret society, the I-ho-ch'üan, "the Society of the Righteous Harmonious Fists," and they killed many missionaries and some diplomats. Many officials sympathized with the Boxers. The officials hated the "Ocean People," those outside barbarians, the Western Powers, who were chopping off pieces of China each for itself, and who were controlling much of China's national income to pay for the wars forced on her and lost. The Boxers said they would drive all of these barbarians into the sea.

In the middle of a class, one day in the late spring of 1900, a teacher appeared at the door of our classroom. She was not the one teaching our class nor yet our form mistress. She looked at our teacher and our teacher looked at her. They did not say a word to each other.

"Mary, will you come with me."

Mary went out of the room and we did not see her again for several days. It was a very subdued Mary whom we next saw.

Almost every day, it seemed, someone was called out of class.

We found it difficult to study. We wanted to look out of the window and watch for the master from the Boys' School coming up the hill to our school. News came first to them. We gathered in knots by the tennis courts, those of us who still had not been called out of the classroom, to watch for him. Who would be next called?

Bena, my special friend, was not at class one day. When next I saw her, her freckles stood out sharply and her eyes looked large. We went for a walk on the terraces. We walked through the garden hand in hand. She did not say anything. I did not say anything. There was no need to say anything. I knew and she knew that I knew. Bena was now alone in the world. Her father and mother and little brothers had all been killed at their mission station by the Boxers.

The fathers and mothers of those other girls had been killed by the Boxers.

The first Westerner killed was Mr. Brooks, a missionary of the English Baptist Mission in the western part of Shantung province, our province. (His bride had put on her wedding dress, the night before their wedding, for me to see, to cheer me, when I had been so ill a couple of winters before.) The Boxers, with red cloth tied around their heads and red sashes around their wists, had killed him. They had tied his hands together and his feet together, and carried him on a pole as they carried their pigs to the butcher, and had cut off his head with one of those choppers the farmers used to cut off the heads of the wheat, bundle by bundle, with a grinding crunch.

How did we know? How do children know?

The Boxers were besieging the legations in Peking. The German minister had been killed, and a secretary from the Japanese legation.

At night we could hear the footsteps of those who were patrolling the schools, little squads in regular beats through the grounds of the three schools and the houses where the teachers lived. They were the masters and the big boys. At the foot of our beds hung the bags we had prepared. Each bag had in it a full set of clothing, underwear, and a dress, and on it was sewed a big number. It was the number of the rowboat we were to go to if the alarm sounded. The teachers were taking no chances of our forgetting to which boat we were each to go. We were told—if the alarm sounded at night—not to wait to dress but to seize the bag, slip our feet into the shoes by the side of the bed, and run as fast as we could to the beach, to the rowboat of our number. The big boys would then row us out to the United States gunboat in the harbor. If the alarm sounded by day we were to drop whatever we were doing and go—as we were, from wherever we were—to the beach and the boats.

Then one day the teacher said to me, "Get your clothes together, your parents are coming for you." I had not even known they were in Chefoo. They took John and me out of school and we all lived in a house on top of Consular Hill, next to the United States consulate. The house had been built as a summer home by an American missionary to Shanghai, who, stranded by the war between the States when his backers in the South could no longer send him money, had gone into business and become wealthy. His daughter gave the house to the Southern Baptist missionaries for a rest home. The Baptist missionaries from all over North China were now living in it as refugees, a family to a room. They had even taken in the rebel Gospel Mission.

Old Dr. Crawford, the leader of those rebels, dressed in a long black alpaca coat—his own design, he said with skirts like a Prince Albert but buttoned all the way down. He claimed that it was also buttoned all the way up, a claim no one could dispute for his heavy iron grey beard covered his throat and his chest. The men of the foreign settlement had formed themselves into relays to patrol the settlement day and night. Dr. Crawford was highly incensed because they would not give him an assignment. Thumping the floor with his cane, he would say to anyone he saw at any time, "I'm not old. I'm seventy years young." And then, thumping even harder with his cane, marking each word with a thump, he would say, "This dynasty will die nasty."

Father and Mother had had no trouble in Huang-hsien but their Chinese friends had begged them to leave. There was no telling when things might burst, and their presence endangered all the Chinese who knew them. Church members were called the "Secondary Hairy Ones" by the Chinese and were hated almost as much as were the Westerners—those people from over the ocean who were trying to change the good old Chinese ways. Other Chinese hated the Secondary Hairy Ones because they were giving up those ways.

So Father on his bicycle and Mother in a chair carried by four bearers had gone the sixty *li* (twenty miles) to P'eng-lai to wait for the little steamer the consuls in Chefoo were sending up the coast for all the missionaries in that end of the province. So trusting were Father and Mother that they travelled separately to P'eng-lai: the chair bearers taking the short cut over the spur of the hills while Father on his bicycle followed the sandy river bed on the hard beaten paths. Some men had thrown a few stones at Father as he passed through a village. Mother learned, when she came back to Huang-hsien a year later, that the chair bearers had had a discussion as they rested and smoked on the bank of the Sandy River. "Shall we throw her in?" "No, she has paid us to take her to P'eng-lai." The contract had been made and they had had their pay, they must now fulfill their end of the bargain. Mother knew, however, that the situation was really desperate when she saw the attitude of the sailors on the Chinese man-of-war, on which the little foreign community had been invited by the Chinese Admiral Sha to wait for the rescue ship. Mother said she carried the baby in her arms along the deck and not one of the sailors smiled or even looked at him. Usually, wherever they went, the Chinese—who all love babies—would chortle and smile with pleasure at one so strange-looking with his yellow curls and blue eyes and white skin, and yet a baby.

With the many families in one house on that hilltop in Chefoo there were more children than usual to play with. Our favorite pastime was watching the sailor from the American gunboat who was on duty at the consulate, watching him wig-wag with his little square flags on short poles, sending the news back and forth from the consulate to the gunboat. The boys even talked with him. This gave them great face with the rest of us children.

The boys brought the news to the elders. "The Allies were repulsed today." Great gloom among the elders. We all knew about the efforts of the small band of Allied soldiers to reach Peking and save the people—diplomats, missionaries, merchants, students—besieged in the Legation quarter.

"The Allies are ten miles from Peking." Rejoicing among the elders.

"The Allies have entered Peking. The siege of the Peking Legations is lifted." Great celebrations among the elders.

We boarded a coastal steamer and went to Shanghai and from there by ocean liner to San Francisco: a month on the great wide ocean, a month to play with other children, Western children of many ages. Our parents said, "Since we cannot go back to our station we might as well take the furlough (one year of rest in seven or eight) that is almost due anyway."

Leaning against the ship's rail in San Francisco I

marvelled at the mountainous horses on the dock. Our
horses in China were Mongolian ponies and these I was
told were Percherons. Fascinated, I watched them lift one
great hoof after another and put it down to shake the
timbers. I wondered to see the longshoremen work without dignity. Labor, I had been taught by precept from
my parents and example by the people around me, was
as honorable as any other occupation. I had been reared
among peasants. One was still a human being and worthy
of self-respect and the respect of others and the dignity of
self-respect. I was shocked to see old age without dignity.
An old man pushing a wheelbarrow. That in itself was
all right. I had seen old peasants collecting animal
droppings for the family fertilizer pile, but I had never
seen gray heads jeered at and the jeers answered.

A year of going from place to place as my parents
made reports of their work in churches, where John and
I, Exhibit A and Exhibit B, dressed in Chinese clothes,
were stood upon the platforms; of visiting relatives I had
heard about and others I had not heard about; of attending
public school for a term in Atlanta, Georgia, where I
learned nothing. I was glad to sit on the back row and
be left alone. I cannot blame the young teacher, who had
all she could do to manage the extroverts in the front
rows.

Among all the people we met, always to me new
ones, there were a few who were friends for longer times.
I saw a boy in Atlanta, a little older than I, sitting on a
stone lion beside the front steps of his home. I knew I
liked him, that he was one to be liked, and found in the
years to come that I had not erred in judgment.

I was glad when the year in America was up and

we were returning home. I was now twelve years old and felt very proud and very grown up that my parents had to buy a full fare ticket for me to cross the ocean, that I could eat with the grown people and did not have to eat at the children's table. In spite, however, of my "grown up" status I continued, all those weeks as we chugged across the wide Pacific, to play with the children of whom, as usual on the steamers going back and forth between China and America, there were many. Even so I knew my childhood was ended and I was entering a new part of my life. I was glad we were returning to our home in the Chinese compound and to the English school in Chefoo. America was still incomprehensible to me. The time to step out into the great world was not yet.

CHINESE MATERIALS CENTER

ASIAN LIBRARY SERIES

Robert L. Irick, General Editor

1. *Translations from Po Chü-i's Collected Works: III, Regulated and Patterned Poems of Middle Age (822-832),* translated and described by Howard S. Levy, rendered by Henry W. Wells (1976), xxxiv, 215pp. ISBN 0-89644-463-5.
2. *Translations From Po Chü-i's Collected Works: IV, The Later Years (833-846),* translated and described by Howard S. Levy, rendered by Henry W. Wells (1978), li, 711pp. ISBN 0-89644-518-6.
3. John Marney, *A Handbook of Modern Chinese Grammar* (1977), 78pp. Paperbound. ISBN 0-89644-464-3.
4. Henry W. Wells, tr., *Diary of a Pilgrim to Ise,* attributed to Saka Jūbutsu, with illustrations by Ch'eng Hsi (1977), xii, 135pp. Paperbound. ISBN 0-89644-501-1.
5. Teng Shou-hsin, *A Basic Course in Chinese Grammar: A Graded Approach through Conversational Chinese* (1977), xii, 135pp. Paperbound. ISBN 0-89644-502-X.
6. George Williams Carrington, *Foreigners in Formosa, 1841-1874* (1977), frontis., map, index, xiv, 308pp. ISBN 0-89644-506-2.
7. Orlan Lee, *Legal and Moral Systems in Asian Customary Law: The Legacy of the Buddhist Social Ethic and Buddhist Law* (1978), map, index, xxiv, 456pp. ISBN 0-89644-524-0.
8. Miao, Ronald C., ed., *Chinese Poetry and Poetics, Vol. 1* (1978), xiv, 375pp. ISBN 0-89644-525-9.
9. Jay Sailey, *The Master Who Embraces Simplicity: A Study of the Chinese Philosopher, Ko Hung, A.D. 283-343* (1978),

index, xxvi, 658pp. ISBN 0-89644-522-4.
10. Ida Pruitt, *A China Childhood* (1978), xi, 205pp. ISBN 0-89644-523-2.
11. Edward A. Kracke, Jr., *Translations of Sung Civil Service Titles, Classification Terms, and Governmental Organ Names*, rev. ed. (1978), xiii, 35pp. ISBN 0-89644-526-7.

IN PREPARATION

Shan-yüan Hsieh, "The Life and Thought of Li Kou, 1009-1059."

Robert L. Irick, "Ch'ing Policy Toward the Coolie Trade, 1847-1878."

Li Yu-hwa, " 'The Last Rite' and Other Stories."

Edward Gerald Martinique, "Chinese Traditional Bookbinding: A Study of its Evolution and Techniques."

Arnold J. Meagher, "Introduction of Chinese Laborers to Latin America: The 'Coolie Trade,' 1847-1874."

Ronald C. Miao, "The Life and Lyric Poetry of Wang Ts'an, 177-217."

Constance Miller, "Technical and Cultural Prerequisites for the Invention of Printing in China and the West."

Shiow-jyu Lu Shaw, "The Imperial Printing of Early Ch'ing China, 1644-1805.

Paul Vander Meer, "Farm-plot Dispersal: Lu-liao Village, Taiwan, 1967."

CHINESE MATERIALS CENTER

RESEARCH AIDS SERIES

Robert L. Irick, General Editor

1. *Research Guide to the* Chiao-hui hsin-pao ("The Church News"), *1868-1874* 敎會新報目錄導要, compiled by Adrian A. Bennett (1975), xviii, 342pp. ISBN 0-89644-528-3.
2. *Research Guide to the* Wan-kuo kung-pao ("The Globe Magazine"), *1874-1883* 萬國公報目錄導要 , compiled by Adrian A. Bennett (1976), xvi, 519pp. ISBN 0-89644-529-1.

CHINESE MATERIALS AND RESEARCH AIDS SERVICE CENTER

RESEARCH AIDS SERIES

Robert L. Irick, General Editor

1. *A Classified Index to Articles on Fiscal Policy (1945-65)* 財政論文分類索引 , compiled by Frank K. S. Yüan 袁坤祥 and Ma Ching-hsien 馬景賢 (1967), xxxvi, 303pp. ISBN 0-89644-540-2.

2. *A Classified Index to Articles on Economics (1945-65)* 經濟論文分類索引 , compiled by Frank K. S. Yüan 袁坤祥 and Ma Ching-hsien 馬景賢 (1967), 2 vols., ciii, (1), 1-792pp. + iii, (1), 793-1,742pp. ISBN 0-89644-541-0.

3. *A Classified Index to Articles on Money and Banking (1945-65)* 貨幣金融論文分類索引, compiled by Frank K. S. Yüan 袁坤祥 and Ma Ching-hsien 馬景賢 (1967), xliii, 329pp. ISBN 0-89644-542-9.

4. *A Concordance to the Poems of Li Ho (790-816)* 李賀詩引得, compiled by Robert L. Irick 艾文博 (1969), xlii, 217pp. ISBN 0-89644-543-7.

5. *A Chinese-Mongolian Dictionary* 漢蒙字典 , compiled by Harnod Hakanchulu 哈勘楚倫 (1969), lxxviii, 1,536pp. ISBN 0-89644-544-5.

6. *A Typeset Edition of the Diary of Weng T'ung-ho with Index* 翁同龢日記排印本附索引 , edited by Chao Chung-fu 趙中孚 (1970). Text in 5 vols., 5, 1-524pp. + 525-993pp. + 995-1,522pp. + 1,523-2,002pp. + 2,003-2,448pp. Index to be announced. ISBN 0-89644-545-3.

7. *Title and Author Index to* Ts'ung-shu *in Taiwan Libraries* 臺灣各圖書館現存叢書子目索引 , compiled by Wang Paohsien 王寶先. Part I: Title Index, 2 vols. (1976), xxi, 868pp.

+ ii, 740pp. Part II: Author Index, (1977), xii, 190pp. ISBN 0-89644-546-1.

8. *A Typeset Edition of the* Tu-li ts'un-i 讀例存疑重刊本, edited by Huang Tsing-chia 黃靜嘉 (1970), 5 vols., 1-262pp. + 4, 1-372pp. + 2, 373-699pp. + 2, 701-1,025pp. + 2, 1,027-1,357pp. ISBN 0-89644-547-X.

9. *A Concordance to the* Kuan-tzu 管子引得, compiled by Wallace Johnson 莊爲斯 (1970), lxxviii, 1,188pp. ISBN 0-89644-548-8.

10. *Index to the Ho Collection of Twenty-Eight* Shih-hua 索引本 何氏歷代詩話, compiled by Helmut Martin 馬漢茂 (1973), 2 vols.: vol. 1, xviii, 533pp.; vol. 2, L, 860pp. ISBN 0-89644-549-6.

11. *A Concordance to the* Kuo-yü 國語引得, compiled by Wolfgang Bauer 包吾剛 (1973), 2 vols.: vol. 1, xlii, 808pp.; vol. 2, iv, 486pp. ISBN 0-89644-550-X.

12. *A Concordance to the* Jen-wu Chih *with a Text* 人物志引得, compiled by Wolfgang Bauer 包吾剛 (1974), xvi, 240pp. ISBN 0-89644-551-8.

13. *A Concordance to* Han-fei Tzu 韓非子引得, compiled by Wallace Johnson 莊爲斯 (1975), xxxix, 978pp. ISBN 0-89644-552-6.

14. *A Concordance to the Poems of Wei Ying-wu* 韋應物詩注引得, compiled by Thomas P. Nielson (1976), lxxii, 220pp. ISBN 0-89644-553-4.

15. *An Index to Sung Dynasty Titles Extant in* Ts'ung-shu 叢書 索引宋文子目, compiled by Brian E. McKnight (1977), xii, 373pp. ISBN 0-89644-554-2.

16. *An Annotated Guide to Documents on Sino-Japanese-Korean Relations in the Late Ch'ing Dynasty* 清季中日韓關係資料 卅種綜合分類目錄, compiled by Li Yü-shu 李毓澍 (1977), 2 vols., xxxii, 1-699pp. + xxxii, 701-1,169pp. ISBN 0-89644-555-0.

17. *Modern Japanese Authors in Area Studies: A Namelist*, compiled by Austin C. W. Shu (1978), xii, 151pp. ISBN 0-89644-517-8.

IN PREPARATION

"A Index to Diplomatic Documents of the Late Ch'ing Dynasty (1875-1911) 清季外交史料引得," compiled by Robert L. Irick 艾文博.

"Index to Chinese Terms in the English Translations of Henry Doré, *Researches into Chinese Superstitions*, vols. 1-10 and 13," compiled by Anne S. Goodrich.

"Chinese Names of Foreigners in China," edited by Robert L. Irick 艾文博 and Linda Marks.

"Taiwan Publications, 1964-1974: An Index by Subject, Author, and Title to New Works and Reprints appearing in CMRASC Booklists," edited by Robert L. Irick.

CHINESE MATERIALS AND RESEARCH AIDS
SERVICE CENTER

OCCASIONAL SERIES

Robert L. Irick, General Editor

1. *An Annotated Guide to Taiwan Periodical Literature, 1966,* edited by Robert L. Irick (1966). Out of print. (See No. 15 below.)
2. *A Ming Directory—1968,* compiled by Ronald Dimberg, Edward L. Farmer, and Robert L. Irick (1968). Out of print.
3. Grace Wan, *A Guide to* Gwoyeu Tsyrdean (1969). Paperbound, 43pp. ISBN 0-89644-134-2.
4. *"Nothing Concealed": Essays in Honor of Liu Yü-yün,* edited by Frederic Wakeman, Jr. (1970), xv, 221pp. ISBN 0-89644-198-9.
5. Wolfram Eberhard, *Sternkunde und Weltbild in Alten China: Gesammelte Aufsätze* (1971), 417pp. ISBN 0-89644-203-9.
6. Wolfram Eberhard, *Moral and Social Values of the Chinese: Collected Essays* (1972), xiv, 506pp. ISBN 0-89644-356-6.
7. David B. Chan, *The Usurpation of the Prince of Yen, 1403-1424* (1976), xi, 173pp. ISBN 0-89644-457-0.
8. *An Author-Title Index to* Ch'üan Han San-kuo Chin Nan Pei-ch'ao shih 全漢三國晉南北朝詩篇名目錄 , compiled by Mei-lan Marney (1973), 160pp. ISBN 0-89644-530-5.
9. *Modern Chinese Authors: A List of Pseudonyms,* compiled by Austin C. W. Shu, 2nd revised and enlarged edition (1973). ISBN 0-89644-531-3.
10. *An Annotated Guide to Current Chinese Periodicals in Hong Kong,* compiled by Paul. P. W. Cheng (1973), xii, 71pp. ISBN 0-89644-358-2.
11. Clarence Burton Day, *Career in Cathay* (1975), 185pp.

ISBN 0-89644-420-1.

12. *Vietnamese, Cambodian, and Laotian Newspapers: An International Union List*, compiled by G. Raymond Nunn and Do Van Anh (1973), xiii, 104pp. ISBN 0-89644-532-1.

13. *Burmese and Thai Newspapers: An International Union List*, compiled by G. Raymond Nunn (1973), xii, 44pp. ISBN 0-89644-533-X.

14. *Indonesian Newspapers: An International Union List*, compiled by G. Raymond Nunn (1973), xv, 131pp. ISBN 0-89644-534-8.

15. *An Annotated Guide to Taiwan Periodical Literature, 1972*, edited by Robert L. Irick (1973), ix, 174pp. ISBN 0-89644-359-0.

16. Chang-kyun Yu, *Sa-seong Thong-ko* or *Ssu-sheng T'ung-k'ao (A Comprehensive Study of Four Tones)* (1973), xxiv, 286pp. ISBN 0-89644-535-6.

17. Chang-kyun Yu, *Meng-ku Yün-lüeh (Abbreviated Chinese Rimes in the Mongolian Script)* (1974), xxxiii, 290pp. ISBN 0-89644-536-4.

18. *An Index to Stories of the Supernatural in the Fa Yüan chu lin* 法苑珠林志怪小說引得, compiled by Jordan D. Paper (1973). Paperbound, ix, 29pp. ISBN 0-89644-537-2.

19. *Translation and Permanence in Chinese History and Culture: A Festschrift in Honor of Dr. Hsiao Kung-ch'üan*, edited by David C. Buxbaum and Frederick W. Mote (1973), xxvi, 433pp. ISBN 0-89644-357-4.

20. *An Index to the Ch'ao-yeh lei-yao* 朝野類要引得, compiled by Stephen Hsing-tao Yü (1974), x, 28pp. Paperbound. ISBN 0-89644-538-0.

21. *Neglected Formosa: A Translation from the Dutch of Frederic Coyett's 't Verwaerloosde Formosa*, edited by Inez de Beauclair (1975), xviii, 207pp. ISBN 0-89644-416-3.

22. Clarence Burton Day, *Peasant Cults in India* (1975), xviii, 126pp. ISBN 0-89644-421-X.

23. Knight Biggerstaff, *Some Early Chinese Steps Toward Modernization* (1975), vii, 107pp. ISBN 0-89644-417-1.

24. Romeyn Taylor, *Basic Annals of Ming T'ai-tsu* (1975), vi, 212pp. ISBN 0-89644-433-3.

25. Sing-wu Wang, *The Organization of Chinese Emigration,*

1848-1888 (1978), xviii, 436pp. ISBN 0-89644-480-5.

26. Chiang Kuei, *The Whirlwind*, translated by Timothy A. Ross (1977), frontis., x, 558pp. ISBN 0-89644-493-7.

27. Ch'en Ku-ying 陳鼓應 , *Lao Tzu: Text, Notes, and Comments*, translated and adapted by Rhett Y.W. Young 楊有維 and Roger T. Ames (1977), viii, 341pp. ISBN 0-89644-520-8.

28. *A Catalog of Kuang-tung Land Records in the Taiwan Branch of the National Central Library*, compiled by Taiwan Branch of the National Central Library, with an introduction by Roy Hofheinz, Jr. (1975), xxvii, 77pp. ISBN 0-89644-439-2.

29. *Studia Asiatica: Essays in Asian Studies in Felicitation of the Seventy-fifth Anniversary of Professor Ch'en Shou-yi*, edited by Laurence G. Thompson (1975), xxvii, 485pp. ISBN 0-89644-476-7.

30. Clarence Burton Day, *Popular Religion in Pre-Communist China* (1975), viii, 102pp. ISBN 0-89644-422-8.

31. Alvin P. Cohen, *Grammar Notes for Introductory Classical Chinese* (1975), 58pp. ISBN 0-89644-419-8.

32. *A Union List of Chinese Periodicals in Universities and Colleges in Taiwan* 中華民國台灣地區大專院校中期刊聯合目錄, compiled by William Ju 諸家駿, xvii, 580pp. ISBN 0-89644-539-9.

33. *Papers in Honor of Professor Woodbridge Bingham: A Festschrift for his Seventy-fifth Birthday*, edited by James B. Parsons (1976), xvi, 286pp. ISBN 0-89644-466-X.

34. *Concordances and Indexes to Chinese Texts*, compiled by D. L. McMullen (1975), x, 204pp. ISBN 0-89644-427-9.

35. Shih Shu-ch'ing, *The Barren Years and Other Short Stories and Plays* (1976), vii, 255pp. ISBN 0-89644-473-2.

36. Clarence Burton Day, *The Indian Interlude* (1977), x, 151pp. 16 pages of photos. ISBN 0-89644-500-3.

37. Clarence Burton Day, *The Birth Pangs of Pakistan* (1977), viii, 141pp. ISBN 0-89644-498-8.

38. Donner, Frederick W., Jr., comp., *A Preliminary Glossary of Chinese Linguistic Terminology* (1977), x, 117p. ISBN 0-89644-521-6.

IN PREPARATION

Allan Frederick Gates, "Christianity and Animism in Taiwan."

John E. Reinecke, "Feigned Necessity: Hawaii's Attempt to Obtain Chinese Contract Labor, 1921-1923."

CHINESE MATERIALS AND RESEARCH AIDS
SERVICE CENTER

BIBLIOGRAPHICAL AIDS SERIES

Robert L. Irick, General Editor

1. *A Checklist of Reference Works in Teng and Biggerstaff Now Available in Taiwan* (1970), 2, 33pp. Paperbound. ISBN 0-89644-199-7.
2. Lei Shu: *Old Chinese Reference Works and a Checklist of Cited Titles Available in Taiwan,* compiled by Austin C. W. Shu (1973), xvii, 37pp. Paperbound. ISBN 0-89644-527-5.
3. *A Descriptive Catalog of the Ming Editions in the Far Eastern Library of the University of Washington,* compiled Chik-fong Lee (1975), xvii, 53pp. Paperbound. ISBN 0-89644-425-2.
4. *Chinese Folk Narratives: A Bibliographical Guide,* compiled by Nai-tung Ting and Lee-hsia Hsü Ting (1975), xiii, 68pp. Paperbound. ISBN 0-89644-434-1.

SERIES COMPLETED

CHINESE MATERIALS CENTER, INC.

Reprint Series

1. Lewis, Ida Belle, *The Education of Girls in China* (San Francisco: CMC, 1974; Repr. of New York: Teachers College, Columbia University, 1919), (xii), 92pp., 1 folding map.
2. Beal, Samuel, intro. and tr., *The Life of Hiuen-Tsiang by the Shaman Hwui Li* (San Francisco: CMC, 1974; Repr. of London: Kegan, Paul, Trench, Trübner & Co., 1911), (ii), xlviii, 218pp.
3. Giles, Herbert A., tr., *Strange Stories from a Chinese Studio* (San Francisco: CMC, 1974; Repr. of London: T. Werner Laurie, 1916), (ii), xxiv, 488pp.
4. Morse, H.B., *In the Days of the Taipings* (San Francisco: CMC, 1974; Repr. of Salem: The Essex Institute 1927), frontis., (iv), xiv, 434pp.
5. Howard, Harvey J., *Ten Weeks with Chinese Bandits* (San Francisco: CMC, 1974; Repr. of New York: Dodd, Mead and Company, 1927), frontis., (ii), xxxiv, 399pp., 1 folding map.
6. Hall, W.H. & W.D. Bernard, *The Nemesis in China* (San Francisco: CMC, 1974; Repr. of London: Henry Colburn, 1847), (iv), xvi 272pp.
7. Thomson, John, *Through China with a Camera* (San Francisco: CMC, 1974; Repr. of Westminister: A. Constable & Co., 1898), (ii), xiv, 284pp.
8. Duyvendak, J.J.L., tr. and ed., *The Book of Lord Shang* (San Francisco: CMC, 1974; Repr. of London: Arthur Probstain, 1928), (ii), xvi, 346pp.
9. Kerr, John Glasgow, *A Guide to the City and Suburbs of Canton* (San Francisco: CMC, 1974; Repr. of Hong Kong: Kelly and Walsh, 1918), viii, 103pp., 1 folding map.
10. Grey, John Henry, *Walks in the City of Canton* (San Francisco: CMC, 1974; Repr. of Hong Kong: De Souza & Co., 1875), (vi), vi, 695, lxipp.
11. des Rotours, Robert, *Traité des fonctionnaires et Traité de*

l'Armee (San Francisco: CMC, 1974; Repr. of 2nd ed.—revised and corrected [Leiden: E.J. Brill, 1948]), cxx, 499 + (iv), 594 (ii)pp., 9 folding maps, 1 folding chart, 2 v.

12. Burns, Islay, *Memoir of the Reverend William C. Burns, M. A., Missionary to China from the English Presbyterian Church* (San Francisco: CMC, 1975; Repr. of New York: Robert Carter and Brothers, 1870), (viii), viii, 595pp.

13. *Report of the Advisory Committee Together with Other Documents Respecting the Chinese Indemnity* (San Francisco: CMC, 1975; Repr. of London: Her Majesty's Stationery Office, 1926), (ii), 197pp.

14. *Report of the Commission of Extraterritoriality in China* (San Francisco: CMC, 1975; Repr. of London: His Majesty's Stationery Office, 1926), (ii), 130pp.

15. Beale, Louis & G. Clinton, *Trade and Economic Conditions in China, 1931-1933, Together with an Annex on Trading Conditions in Manchuria* (San Francisco: CMC, 1975; Repr. of London: His Majesty's Stationery Office, 1933), (ii), 174pp., 1 folding map.

16. *Report on the Trade of Central and Southern China* (San Francisco: CMC, 1975; Repr. of London: His Majesty's Stationery Office, 1898), (ii), 99pp.

17. *Papers Relating to the Riot in Canton in July 1846 and to the Proceedings Against Mr. Compton, a British Subject, for His Participation in That Riot* (San Francisco: CMC, 1975; Repr. of London: T.R. Harrison, 1847), (ii), vi, 130pp.

18. *Correspondence Respecting Insults in China* (San Francisco: CMC, 1975; Repr. of London: Harrison and Sons, 1857), (ii), viii, 228pp.

19. *Correspondence Respecting Anti-foreign Riots in China, 1891-1892* (San Francisco: CMC, 1975; Repr. of London: Her Majesty's Stationery Office, 1891), (iv), 176pp.

20. *Correspondence Respecting the Attack on British Protestant Missionaries at Yang-chow-foo, August 1868* (San Francisco: CMC, 1975; Repr. of London: Harrison and Sons, 1869), (ii), iv, 78, (4), 18pp.

21. *Correspondence Respecting the Attack on the Indian Expedition to Western China, and the Murder of Mr. Margary*

(San Francisco: CMC, 1975; Repr. of London: Harrison and Sons, 1876, 1877), (ii), iv, 148pp.

22. *Papers Relating to the Rebellion in China and Trade in the Yang-tze-kiang River* (San Francisco: CMC, 1975; Repr. of London: Harrison and Sons, 1862), (ii), iv, 158pp. 1 folding map.

23. *Further Papers Relating to the Rebellion in China* (San Francisco: CMC, 1975; Repr. of London: Harrison and Sons, 1863), (iv), 196pp.

24. Hamberg, Theodore, *The Visions of Hung-siu-tshuen and Origin of the Kwang-si Insurrection* (San Francisco: CMC, 1975; Repr. of Hong Kong: China Mail Office, 1854), (iv), vi, 63, (i), xiipp.

25. *Foreign Relations of the United States, 1901: Affairs in China. Report of William W. Rockhill, Late Commissioner to China, with Accompanying Documents* (San Francisco: CMC, 1975; Repr. of China reprint edition, 1941), (ii), 391pp.

26. *Correspondence Respecting the Revision of the Treaty of Tien-tsin* (San Francisco: CMC, 1975; Repr. of London: Harrison and Sons, 1871), (ii), viii, 467pp.

27. Allman, Norwood F., *Handbook on the Protection of Trade-marks, Patents, Copyrights, and Trade-names in China* (San Francisco: CMC, 1975; Repr. of Shanghai: Kelly & Walsh, 1924), (vi), iv, 207, 5pp.

28. Hsia, Ching-lin, *Studies in Chinese Diplomatic History* (San Francisco: CMC, 1975; Repr. of Shanghai: Commercial Press, 1925), (ii) xii, 266, 4pp.

29. Song Ong Siang, *One Hundred Years' History of the Chinese in Singapore; Being a Chronological Record of the Contribution by the Chinese Community to the Development, Progress and Prosperity of Singapore; of Events and Incidents Concerning the Whole or Sections of That Community and of the Lives, Pursuits and Public Service of Individual Members Thereof from the Foundation of Singapore on 6th February 1919* (San Francisco: CMC, 1975; Repr. of London: John Murray, 1923), (iv), xxii, 602pp.

30. Sargent, A.J., *Anglo-Chinese Commerce and Diplomacy (Mainly in the Nineteenth Century)* (San Francisco: CMC,

1975; Repr. of Oxford: Clarendon Press, 1907), frontis., xii, 332pp.

31. Rasmussen, O.D., *What's Right with China: An Answer to Foreign Criticisms* (San Francisco: CMC, 1975; Repr. of Shanghai: Commercial Press, 1927), (ii), xx, 255pp.

32. Soothill, W.E., *China and the West: A Sketch of Their Intercourse* (San Francisco: CMC, 1975; Repr. of London: Humphrey Milford, 1925), frontis., (iv), viii, 216pp.

33. Arnold, Jolean, et al., *Commercial Handbook of China* (San Francisco: CMC, 1975; Repr. of US Dept. of Commerce, Bureau of Foreign and Domestic Commerce, Miscellaneous Series No. 84 [Washington: Government Printing Office, 1919]), frontis., (ii), 630pp., 2 folding maps. + frontis., (ii), 470pp. 2v.

34. *Further Correspondence Respecting the Disturbances in China* (San Francisco: CMC, 1975; Repr. of London: His Majesty's Stationery Office, 1901), (ii), xxiv, 200 + (ii), xv, (i), 175pp.

35. *Correspondence Relative to the Earl of Elgin's Special Missions to China and Japan, 1857-1859* (San Francisco: CMC, 1975; Repr. of London: Harrison and Sons, 1859), (ii), xii, 488pp.

36. Legge, James, tr., *A Record of Buddhistic Kingdoms: Being an Account by the Chinese Monk Fa-Hien of His Travels in India and Ceylon (A.D. 399-414) in Search of the Buddhist Books of Discipline* (San Francisco: CMC, 1975; Repr. of Oxford: Clarendon Press, 1886), (iv), vx, (i), 123, (45)pp., 1 folding map.

37. Tucci, G., *On Some Aspects of the Doctrines of Maitreya [Nātha] and Asaṅga (Being a Course of Five Lectures Delivered at the University of Calcutta)* (San Francisco: CMC, 1975; Repr. of Calcutta: Univ. of Calcutta, 1930), (viii), 82, 2pp.

38. Watters, Thomas, *On Yuan Chwang's Travels in India, 629-645 A.D.* (San Francisco: CMC, 1975; Repr. of London: Royal Asiatic Society, 1904), (ii), xvi, 401 + vi, 357pp., 2 folding maps. 2v.

39. Nanjio, Bunyiu, *A Catalogue of the Chinese Buddhist Tri-*

pitaka: the Sacred Canon of the Buddhists in China and Japan (San Francisco: CMC, 1975; Repr. of Oxford: Clarendon Press, 1893), xxxvi, 480 columns.

40. Beal, Samuel, Si-yu-ki: *Buddhist Records of the Western World; Translated from the Chinese of Hiuen Tsiang (A.D. 629)* (San Francisco: CMC, 1976; Repr. of London: Kegan Paul, Trench, Trübner & Co., n.d.), (ii), cxii, 242 + viii, 369pp. 2v. in 1.

41. Rockhill, W. Woodville, tr., *The Life of the Buddha and the Early History of His Order; Derived from Tibetan Works in the* Bkah-Hgyur *and* Bstan-Hgyur; *Followed by Notices on the Early History of Tibet and Khoten* (San Francisco: CMC, 1976; Repr. of London: Kegan Paul, Trench, Trübner & Co., Introduction dated June 1884), xii, 273pp.

42. Edkins, Joseph, *Chinese Buddhism: A Volume of Sketches, Historical, Descriptive, and Critical* (San Francisco: CMC, 1976; Repr. of Trübner's Oriental Series, 2nd rev. ed. [London: Kegan Paul, Trench, Trübner, & Co., 1893]), (ii), xxxiv, 453pp.

43. Grousset, Réné, *In the Footsteps of the Buddha*, tr. from the French by Mariette Leon (San Francisco: CMC, 1976; Repr. of London: George Routledge & Sons, 1932), (ii), xii, 352pp., 2 folding maps.

44. Mateer, A.H., *Siege Days: Personal Experiences of American Women and Children During the Peking Siege* (San Francisco: CMC, 1976; Repr. of New York: Fleming H. Revell Co., 1903), (ii), 411pp.

45. Eitel, Ernest J., *Hand-book of Chinese Buddhism; Being a Sanskrit-Chinese Dictionary with Vocabularies of Buddhist Terms in Pali, Singhalese, Siamese, Burmese, Tibetan, Mongolian and Japanese* (San Francisco: CMC, 1976; Repr. of 2nd rev. and enl. ed. [Tokyo: Sanshusha, 1904]), (x), 324pp.

46. Suzuki, Teitaro, *Acvaghosha's Discourse on the Awakening of Faith in the Mathâyâna* 大乘起信論 (San Francisco: CMC, 1976; Repr. of Chicago: Open Court Publishing Co., 1900), (ii), xviii, 160pp.

47. Taam, Cheuk-Woon 譚卓垣, *The Development of Chinese*

Libraries under the Ch'ing Dynasty, 1644-1911 清代圖書館
發展史 (San Francisco: CMC, 1977; Repr. of Shanghai,
1935), ix, 107pp.

48. Johnston, Reginald Fleming, *Buddhist China* (San Francisco:
CMC, 1976; Repr. of London: John Murray, 1913), (vi),
xviii, 403pp.

49. des Rotours, Robert, *Le Traité des Examens, Traduit de la
Nouvelle Histoire des T'ang (Chap. XLIV, XLV)* (San
Francisco: CMC, 1976; Repr. of 2nd ed.—revised and corrected [Paris: Librairie Ernest Leroux, 1932]), (ii), xii,
417pp.

50. Tucci, Giuseppe, *Pre-Dinnāga Buddhist Texts on Logic from
Chinese Sources* (San Francisco: CMC, 1976; Repr. of
Gaekwad's Oriental Series No. XLIX [Baroda: Oriental
Institute, 1929]), (viii), xxx, 338pp.

51. Tucci, Giuseppe, *The Nyāyamukha of Dignāga, the Oldest
Buddhist Text on Logic, After Chinese and Tibetan Materials*
(San Francisco: CMC, 1976; Repr. of Heidelberg: O. Har-
rassowitz, 1930), (vi), 72pp.

52. Rosenberg, Otto, *Die Probleme der Buddhistischen Philo-
sophie*, tr. by E. Rosenberg (San Francisco: CMC, 1976;
Repr. of Heidelberg: O. Harrassowitz, 1924), (ii), xvi, 287pp.

53. Kitayama, Junyu, *Metaphysik des Buddhismus, Versuch
Einer Philosophischen Interpretation der Lehre Vasubandhus
und Seiner Schule* (San Francisco: CMC, 1976; Repr. of
Stuttgart, Berlin: Verlag Von W. Kohlhammer, 1934), (ii),
xvi, 268pp.

54. Waldschmidt, Ernst, *Gandhara Kutscha Turfan, Eine Ein-
führung in die Frühmittelalterliche Kunst Zentralasiens* (San
Francisco: CMC, 1976; Repr. of Leipzig: Klinkhardt &
Biermann, 1925), (ii), 116pp., 66 pages of photos.

55. Sōgen, Yamakami, *Systems of Buddhistic Thought* (San
Francisco: CMC, 1976; Repr. of Calcutta: University of
Calcutta, 1912), (ii), xx, 316, xxxvipp.

56. von Zach, E., tr., *Yang Hsiung's Fa-yen (Worte Strenger
Ermahnung) ein Philosophischer Traktat aus dem Beginn der
Christlichen Zeitrechnung* (San Francisco: CMC, 1976;
Repr. of Sinologische Beiträge IV [Batavia: Drukkerij Lux,

1939]), (viii), 74pp.

57. Pfister, Louis, *Notices Biographiques et Bibliographiques sur les Jesuites de l'Ancienne Mission de Chine, 1552-1773* (San Francisco: CMC, 1976; Repr. of Variétés Sinologiques Nos. 59 & 60 [Shanghai: Imprimerie de la Mission Catholique, 1932, 1934]), (vi), xxvi, 561, 6 + (vi), x, 547, 38pp. 2v. in 1.

58. Beal, Samuel, tr., *Texts from the Buddhist Canon, Commonly Known as Dhammapada, with Accompanying Narratives* (San Francisco: CMC, 1977; Repr. of Boston: Houghton, Osgood & Co., 1878), (iv), viii, 176pp.

59. Nyanatiloka, *Buddhist Dictionary: Manual of Buddhist Terms and Doctrines* (San Francisco: CMC, 1977; Repr. of Island Hermitage Publication No. 1 [Colombo: Frewin & Co., 1950]), (vi), vi, 190pp., 1 folding diagram.

60. McGovern, William Montgomery, *A Manual of Buddhist Philosophy, Vol. I Cosmology* (San Francisco: CMC, 1977; Repr. of London: Kegan Paul, Trench, Trübner & Co., New York: E.P. Dutton & Co., 1923), (x), 205pp.

61. Soothill, W.E., *The Lotus of the Wonderful Law or the Lotus Gospel: Saddharma Pundarika Sūtra, Miao-fa Lien Hua Ching* (San Francisco: CMC, 1977; Repr. of Oxford: Clarendon Press: 1930), frontis., (ii), xii, 275pp.

62. Herrmann, Albert, *Die Alten Seidenstraſsen Zwischen China und Syrien: Beiträge zur Alten Geographie Asiens, I. Abteilung, Einleitung, die Chinesischen Quellen, Zentralasien nach Ssĕ-ma Tsᶜien und den Annalen der Han-Dynastie* (San Francisco: CMC, 1977; Repr. of Berlin: Weidmannsche Buchhandlung: 1910), (ii), viii, 130pp., 1 folding map.

63. Wilson, Andrew, *The "Ever-Victorious Army": A History of the Chinese Campaign under Lt.-Col. G. G. Gordon, C. B. R. E., and of the Suppression of the Tai-Ping Rebellion.* A Reprint Edition with Marginal Notes by Capt. John Holland (San Francisco: CMC, 1977; Repr. of Edinburgh & London: William Blackwood and Sons: 1868), (vi), xxxii, 396 + 397-410pp., 1 folding map.

64. Ui, H., *The Vaiśesika Philosophy According to the Daśapadārtha-Śāstra: Chinese Text, with Introduction, Translation,*

and Notes, ed. by F. W. Thomas (San Francisco: CMC, 1977; Repr. of Oriental Translation Fund, New Series Vol. xxiv [London: Royal Asiatic Society: 1917]), (iv), xii, 265pp.

65. Waddell, L. Austine, *The Buddhism of Tibet or Lamaism, with Its Mystic Cults, Symbolism and Mythology, and in Its Relation to Indian Buddhism* (San Francisco: CMC, 1977; Repr. of London: W.H. Allen & Co., 1895), frontis., (ii), xx, 598pp.

66. Medhurst, W. H., *The Foreigner in Far Cathay* (San Francisco: CMC, 1977; Repr. of London: Edward Stanford, 1872), (xii), 192pp., 1 map.

67. Dennys, N. B., ed., *The Treaty Ports of China and Japan: A Complete Guide to the Open Ports of Those Countries, Together with Peking, Yedo, Hongkong, and Macao, Forming a Guide Book & Vade Mecum for Travellers, Merchants, and Residents in General* (San Francisco: CMC, 1977; Repr. of London: Trübner and Co., 1867), (iv), viii, (2), 668pp., x1, 26 appendixes, 24 folding maps, 4 maps, 1 diagram.

68. Der Ling, Princess, *Two Years in the Forbidden City* (San Francisco: CMC, 1977; Repr. of New York: Moffat, Yard & Co., 1912), frontis., (ii), ix, (5) 383pp., 17 pl.

69. Broomhall, Marshall, *The Bible in China* (San Francisco: CMC, 1977; Repr. of London: The Religious Tract Society, 1934), (vi), xvi, 190, (2)pp.

70. Bryson, Mary F., *John Kenneth Mackenzie, Medical Missionary to China* (San Francisco: CMC, 1977; Repr. of London: Hodder & Stoughton, 1891), frontis., (iv), xv, (1), 404pp.

71. Stauffer, Milton T., *The Christian Occupation of China: A General Survey of the Numerical Strength and Geographical Distributon[sic] of the Christian Forces in China, Made by the Special Committee on Survey and Occupation, China Continuation Committee, 1918-1921* (San Francisco: CMC, 1977; Repr. of Shanghai: China Continuation Committee, 1922), (vi), 14, 469, cxiipp.

72. MacGillivray, D., *A Century of Protestant Missions in China (1807-1907), Being the Centenary Conference Historical Volume* (San Francisco: CMC, 1977; Repr. of Shanghai:

American Presbyterian Mission Press, 1907), (iv), viii, 678, x1, 52pp., 1 map.

73. *Musings of a Chinese Mystic: Selections from the Philosophy of Chuang Tzu*, with an Introduction by Lionel Giles (San Francisco: CMC, 1977; Repr. of the Wisdom of the East Series [London: John Murray, n.d.]), (ii), 112pp.

74. Mullie, Jos., *The Structural Principles of the Chinese Language, An Introduction to the Spoken Language (Northern Pekingese Dialect)*, tr. by A. Omer Versichel (San Francisco: CMC, 1977; Repr. of Peiping: the Bureau of Engraving & Printing, 1932), (viii), xxxiv, 566, (2)pp., 1 chart. + (viii), 691, (2) pp. 2v.

75. Guinness, M. Geraldine, *The Story of the China Inland Mission* (San Francisco: CMC, 1977; Repr. of London: Morgan & Scott, 1897, 1900), frontis., (iv), xviii, 476pp., 1 folding map. + (iv), xii, 512pp., 1 folding map. 2v.

76. Broomhall, Marshall, *The Jubilee Story of the China Inland Mission, with Portraits, Illustrations & Map* (San Francisco: CMC, 1977; Repr. of London: Morgan & Scott, 1915), frontis., (iv), xvi, 386pp., 1 folding map.

77. De Groot, J. J. M., *Les Fêtes Annuellement Célébrées à Émoui (Amoy), Étude Concernant la Religion Populaire des Chinois*, tr. by C. G. Chavannes, Annales du Musée Guimet Tome Douzième, with a new Introduction by Inez de Beauclair and Harvey Molé (San Francisco: CMC, 1977; Repr. of Paris: Ernest Leroux, Editeur, 1886), frontis., xxiv, xxvi, 400pp. + frontis., (iv), vi, 401-832pp., 24 illus. 2v.

78. Hedin, Sven, *Across the Gobi Desert*, tr. H. J. Cant (San Francisco: CMC, 1977; Repr. of New York: E. P. Dutton & Company, 1932), frontis., (iv), 402pp., 114 illus., 1 map, 2 folding maps.

ROUGH SKETCH OF
SUNG- CHIA- TAN

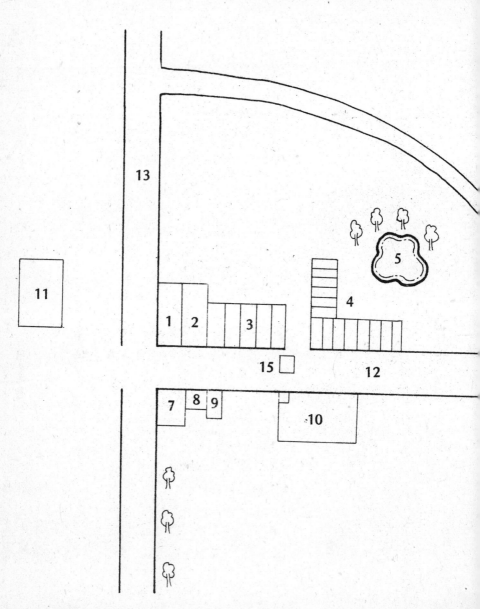